# 150

FOR COUPLES
—AT—
EVERY STAGE

## Unforgettable

# DATES

## HALEY MILLER

### PLAIN SIGHT PUBLISHING
AN IMPRINT OF CEDAR FORT, INC.
SPRINGVILLE, UTAH

ISBN 13: 978-1-4621-1269-2

Published by Plain Sight Publishing, an imprint of Cedar Fort, Inc.
2373 W. 700 S., Springville, UT 84663
Distributed by Cedar Fort, Inc., www.cedarfort.com

LIBRARY OF CONGRESS CATALOGING-IN-PUBLICATION DATA

Miller, Haley, 1988- author.
150 unforgettable dates : for couples at every stage / Haley Miller.
    pages cm
Includes bibliographical references and index.
Summary: A collection of date ideas for couples of all ages.
ISBN 978-1-4621-1269-2 (alk. paper)
1.  Dating (Social customs) 2.  Single people--Recreation. 3.  Amusements.  I. Title.

HQ801.M5674 2014
306.73--dc23

                          2013043184

Cover and interior design by Angela D. Baxter
Cover design © 2014 by Lyle Mortimer
Edited by Whitney Lindsley

Printed in the United States of America

10  9  8  7  6  5  4  3  2  1

Printed on acid-free paper

**TO JARED,**

my absolute-everything buddy

# Contents

# Introduction

*Dating.* Is there any other word in the English language that simultaneously produces so much excitement and so much dread? A good date can have us walking on air and hardly sleeping at night as we wonder what the other person is feeling. A bad date, on the other hand, can leave us swearing off relationships permanently. Sometimes bad dates are simply the result of conflicting personality traits, ideologies, or life goals. In these cases, I'm afraid we can't do much but be considerate and gracious, and then politely decline a second meeting. But other times bad dates are the result of poor planning or a lack of creativity—and that is just what I'm out to rectify.

Dating is first and foremost about getting to know another person, so sitting silently beside each other at the movies or careening down the ski slopes with your date 300 yards behind just doesn't cut it. The activities you engage in should be fun, to be sure, but they should also be useful for discovering what type of person your partner is—how adventurous or creative is he, or what makes her laugh the hardest? Does she love animals? Sports? Trying new things? What is his family like, or what are her personal goals?

This book focuses on the getting-to-know-each-other philosophy of dating by suggesting activities that are conducive to conversation and that help to gently coax subtle character traits and tastes out of your partner. You'll also find helpful talking points, movie and menu recommendations, and adaptations for group and low-budget dates.

Finally, and at the risk of sounding like your mother, I'd like to give you one final bit of dating advice: Be yourself. You are impressive, interesting, and worthwhile, and the right person will see that. Don't be discouraged if a date bombs—take a look at Plan B dates, have the presence of mind to laugh about it, and remember that people progress at different rates. Most important, have fun and try new things so that you can look back on this time in your life (whenever that is!) and say it was one of the best.

# OUTDOORS & NATURE

# 1.

## Sunrise Sweetie

### $0–$25

**THE WHAT:** Pick a Saturday when you don't have anything else planned and tell your date to set her alarm for the crack of dawn—you're going on a hike! Find a hiking path that's close by (if it's a far drive, you'll have to get up even earlier!) and has a decent elevation gain that will give you a good view of the rising sun. Walk slowly and get to know each other on the way up. At the top, sit back, pull out ready-made breakfast foods like granola bars and fruit, and enjoy the light show and each other's company. Or, if you're feeling fancy, stop for breakfast at a café on the way home.

**THE WHY:** It takes someone adventurous to get up before the sun does, and this date is a great way to gauge how "game" your prospective partner is. You can adapt the activity and pick relatively short hikes if you're worried about running out of things to talk about, or longer ones if you're feeling more confident. You can also opt for a sunset hike instead.

 **TALKING TIPS:** Ask your date about any other times she's seen the sunrise, about her favorite experiences in nature, or about what her perfect day would be like.

 **REMINDERS:** The sun rises in the east and sets in the west, so make sure to end your hike facing the correct direction. Always take yours and your date's fitness and physical limitations into consideration when planning potentially strenuous activities.

# 2. "Canoe"dling

$0–$80

**THE WHAT:** Rent or borrow a canoe or sea kayaks and head for the nearest lake or coastline. Paddle around, talk, splash each other, and swap adventure stories. If it's hot, go for a dip in the refreshing water. End with a prepacked picnic lunch on the shore after working up your appetites.

**THE WHY:** If you're in a canoe or two-person kayak, you have a great chance to see how you work as a team and how compatible your communication styles are. If you're in separate kayaks, you have the advantage of being able to stay side by side and get some quality conversation in between the paddling.

 **THE PUNNY PICKUP LINE:** Canoe be mine?

 **REMINDERS:** Plan for the weather and let your date know ahead of time what clothing and footwear is appropriate for the activity.

# 3.

## You Rock My World
### $20–$300

**THE WHAT:** Get beyond boring by taking your date rock climbing! Indoor courses have a one-stop shop for rental gear and are generally the cheapest and most convenient option, often offering both hourly and full-day passes. Renting your own gear or joining a guided group for an outdoor adventure is another possibility, but both are significantly more expensive than a visit to the climbing gym.

**THE WHY:** The old adage that opposites attract may be true for some couples, but it never hurts to have some of the same interests. If you love sports or the outdoors, chances are you'd want to enjoy those things with your significant other without her complaining or being bored. This activity is high adventure without requiring too much skill or experience, and it's an excellent way to get a feel for whether your date is willing to branch out and try new things.

 **BONUS:** Belaying for each other will build trust. And if you do accidentally let your date fall, you can bond during the ambulance ride to the hospital.

 **REMINDERS:** A date is not the time to flaunt your athletic abilities, especially if that means leaving your date at the bottom of the climbing wall while you race to the top. By sticking by your partner's side, you'll be able to make meaningful conversation and get familiar as you give her a hand or a leg up.

# 4. Biking Bliss

## $0–$40

**THE WHAT:** Rent or borrow a tandem bicycle and take a tour of your city or a bike trail together. Plan your route based on sites you want to see, or ride aimlessly until you're both tired—whatever suits your fancy. Take turns being in the front so you both get a feel for being in control. Tandem bikes are usually rented by the hour, so plan accordingly. If you've borrowed the bike or money isn't an issue, ride to a park and stop for a prepacked picnic lunch.

**THE WHY:** Exercise feels good and loosens people up, making it a great way to get comfortable with your date. It can be difficult for the rear rider to hear the person in the front, so conversation is sometimes limited. However, frequent stops along your way and taking turns sitting in the back can resolve this issue. Besides, constant conversation isn't necessary to enjoy yourself and your company when you have the added bonus of soaking in the beautiful scenery.

**GET YOUR GROUP ON:** Go the extra mile—literally! Plan a "Tour de (your city here)" and invite other couples to have a tandem bike race along a planned route. Present medals or prizes to the winners, and then have fun comparing your wrong turns and close calls with pedestrians with the other participants' experiences.

# 5. Sweet Pea

$0–$15

**THE WHAT:** Volunteer to weed or help plant new crops at a community garden. Bring your own gloves and spade, or borrow or buy some, and spend a couple of hours getting to know each other as you make the world a better place. If you're allowed, grab some produce to take home and go back to your place and cook it up to enjoy the fruits (or vegetables) of your labors.

**THE WHY:** See if your date isn't afraid to get his hands a little dirty! A strong work ethic and a willingness to do manual labor likely mean that your partner is down-to-earth and practical—two qualities that come in handy as a relationships get more complicated and honest communication becomes increasingly important.

 **TALKING TIPS:** Find out if your partner has the green-thumb gene—did his grandmother or mother keep a garden? What activities did he most enjoy sharing with grandparents and parents? Talk about favorite family bonding experiences and try to put the memories and emotions into words.

# 6. You're a Cache!

$0

**THE WHAT:** Geocaching became a favorite small-thrills pastime in the early 2000s as GPS technology became readily available. It consists of typing coordinates in to a GPS device or smartphone and searching in that area for a small hidden object that usually contains a scroll of paper where you can record your name once you've found it. Search on geocaching.com for geocaches in your area. Once you've picked a few to search for, write down their coordinates and then use the device of your choice to help lead you to them. Be prepared to squat, bend, dig, climb, and any number of other uncomfortable actions in pursuit of the geocaches—people can be awfully clever when hiding them.

**THE WHY:** You'll get to experience teamwork with your prospective partner as you work together to find the caches. The thrill of the chase and the sense of accomplishment once you've located it hearkens back to the days of treasure maps and buried booty, and you'll both have fun playing pirates for the day.

 **BONUS:** If you're in a steady relationship, geocaching is a date that can be used again and again because each cache is totally different. See how many local caches you can get your name on!

 **REMINDERS:** Some geocache courses get muddy, wet, or rugged, so make sure to let your date know what clothing and footwear is appropriate beforehand.

# 7.

## Let's Go Fly a Kite
### $5–$50

**THE WHAT:** Pick a blustery day and head for the beach or other scenic location (a park will do just fine) and fly kites. You can pick up cheap plastic ones from the dollar or drugstore, or spring for nicer nylon kites from a sporting goods store. Buy one for the two of you to share or get two so you each have your own. Alternatively, you can make a basic kite out of butcher paper, crossed wooden sticks, and twine. If you go that route, have fun painting or personalizing your kites before you fly them.

**THE WHY:** Flying kites is a mellow, soothing activity that often reminds people of childhood or lazy days spent with family. No skill or effort is involved, so it's an easy way to talk to each other while still feeling like you're *doing* something.

**TALKING TIPS:** Did your date fly kites as a kid? What does she do to relax or unwind after a stressful day? What is her favorite type of weather, and why?

# 8. Totally Tubular

$0–$20

**THE WHAT:** In the summer, float down a river or a wide stream in inner tubes. Borrow two from a friend or pick them up for cheap at a general store. Tie them together so you and your date can float along lazily together and talk, splash, and enjoy the good weather.

**THE WHY:** The forward motion of the water will give your conversation some forward motion too. Since the scenery is constantly changing, you can always find something new to talk about. Plus, the look on your date's face when you get sneaky and push him off of his tube will be priceless.

 **REMINDERS:** Have a backup plan in case the weather does not cooperate (see Plan B dates on page 107 for ideas).

 **GET YOUR GROUP ON:** The more the merrier with a fun outdoor activity like this! Invite other couples along and tie yourselves into a giant inner tube chain. Start splash wars and bring squirt guns for extra fun.

# 9.  Go Fish

$0–$80

**THE WHAT:** Bad winter weather doesn't have to mean the end of your adventures in nature! Bundle up and take your date ice fishing at a nearby frozen lake. The sport can be dangerous and requires specialized equipment, so it's recommended that you go with an experienced friend or sign up for a beginner's class and go with a group. Bring hot cocoa in a thermos and pack plenty of snacks. If you end up catching something, clean and gut it, and take it home to cook or freeze and prepare for dinner another night—on a second date, perhaps?

**THE WHY:** Whether you're a student, employed full time, or between jobs, it's easy to get stuck in the routine of your typical day. It's important to challenge yourself to try new things, and to hold your partner to the same standard. Don't get bogged down by the mundane day-to-day—get out and really experience life together!

 **REMINDERS:** You'll be on a frozen lake, so it goes without saying that you need to dress very warmly. Wool socks and gloves, hats, scarves, heavy coats, and two layers on your legs should do the trick. Advise your date to take the same precautions.

 **TALKING TIPS:** As with any fishing trip, it could take hours to get a bite, so only undertake this date with someone you feel fairly comfortable talking to for that long. There won't be much else to do, unless you bring a set of cards, so come prepared to really get to know each other.

# 10. Funky Spelunking

$0–$30

**THE WHAT:** Come on, admit it, you've always wanted to use the word *spelunking* in a sentence. After this date, you'll be throwing it around in conversation like a pro. Spelunking is just a fancy word for cave exploration—all you need is a cave, a good pair of shoes, and some flashlights or headlamps, and you're ready for your next adventure. Every cave is different, and it can be a blast to explore uncharted territory. Research your cave of choice before you go—some are more difficult to navigate than others and can get dangerous, and some state or national parks require a fee.

**THE WHY:** Many caves can be explored in an hour or two, making spelunking a quick and cheap but unique date. There's no need to shell out hundreds of dollars for rafting tours or a hot air balloon ride—you can find adventure that's much easier on your wallet and much closer to home.

 **REMINDERS:** Caves can be slippery, jagged, or very narrow, so caution should always be exercised when exploring them. Make sure that you have plenty of light sources and watch your step carefully.

# 11.

## Holistic Hot Tubbing
### $0–$15

**THE WHAT:** Many states have natural hot springs that are a great landmark to hike to and a fun and more romantic alternative to the hot tub at your apartment complex. Plan to go in the evening when the temperature cools down a bit so you'll enjoy the warmth of the water. Learn about the geologic features that created the springs and impress your date with your smarts. Note that some state and national parks may charge for use of the springs.

**THE WHY:** Hot tubs are an intimate setting where people chill out and let their hair down. A scenic hike followed by a relaxing dip in the springs serves the same purpose—getting to know each other better in an easy, one-on-one environment.

 **REMINDERS:** You and your date will need sturdy hiking shoes and comfortable clothes for the walk to the springs, but will need swimsuits, towels, and flip-flops once there. Plan accordingly by packing backpacks with the necessities.

 **GET YOUR GROUP ON:** If you're still in the early stages of dating this particular partner, you can tone down the intimacy factor of this activity by inviting a few other couples along. As a bonus, if you fill up one of the springs with people that you know, you're less likely to get stuck sitting next to a potentially nude stranger.

# 12. Ice, Ice Baby

## $10

**THE WHAT:** The grass is always greener on the other side, and this is particularly true of weather. In the winter we long for sunny days, and in the summer we miss the refreshing chill of snowfall. Well, who says you can't have both? Give your date Christmas in July by taking him ice blocking! Buy blocks of ice at the grocery store, grab a couple of towels, and find a steep hill. With the towel between you and the ice, take a seat and shove off—you'll get to experience that winter thrill while working on your tan!

**THE WHY:** Ice blocking is quick, cheap, and always fun. There's no better way to get comfortable with someone than by laughing with him. (Or at him—for extra fun, film your runs down the hill, as you're almost guaranteed to fall off a time or two, and you can keep laughing even after the sledding is over as you watch the "America's Funniest Videos"–worthy footage.)

 **REMINDERS:** You will likely get some bumps, bruises, and grass stains from this activity, so make sure you know your date is game before you put him in a situation he doesn't want to be in.

 **FILM FANATICS:** After you've had your ice blocking fill, go back to your place and watch *Cool Runnings,* which is a movie about an Olympic bobsled team from the tropical country of Jamaica. A fitting topic, wouldn't you say?

# FOOD & DRINK

# 13. Wacky Jack-o'-Lanterns
## $2–$15

**THE WHAT:** Who says you have to wait 'til Halloween to make jack-o'-lanterns? Pumpkins may only be in stock in October, but other fruits and vegetables carve up just as easily, and their unique shapes give each jack-o'-lantern a personalized flair. Stock up on squash, eggplant, watermelon, or any other produce with a thick outer shell, get a couple of carving knives, and go to town. You know the drill—have fun making faces or creating characters or scenes with the produce as your canvas. When you're done, make a meal out of the innards and display your creations on your front porch or entryway for your neighbors to wonder about. They'll be jealous they didn't think of it first!

**THE WHY:** Dating can get complicated fast. The more you get to know about someone, the more factors there are in determining whether or not your relationship will work in the long run. That's why it's important to have fun and take things easy, especially at first. A lighthearted, simple date like this is also a great way for established couples to break free from their routine and savor each other's company again.

 **TALKING TIPS:** Ask your date about his favorite Halloween traditions. What was the best costume he ever wore? Did he ever pull pranks? What about other holiday traditions?

 **GET YOUR GROUP ON:** Make this date into a produce-carving contest by inviting other couples to join you and asking a neighbor or passerby to be the unbiased judge. Have a prize for the winners, and enjoy cooking up and snacking on whatever you can make out of the gutted fruits and vegetables.

# 14. Camping Cuisine
### $10–$15

**THE WHAT:** Sometime before the date, buy all of the ingredients for foil dinners and dessert. If your partner likes cooking, begin your date by assembling the foil dinners together. If not, have them ready to go before the date begins. Build a fire at a local park or campground, or in a fire pit in your backyard. Place the foil packets in the fire, turning occasionally. Talk or read ghost stories while you wait for them to finish. After dinner, finish the night off with dessert! S'mores are always an easy option, but a quick web search will produce tons of great alternatives!

**THE WHY:** Something magical happens around the warmth and security of campfires—people feel safe and will often open up in new ways around such a comforting environment, allowing you to have new and meaningful conversations with your partner. And the delicious food never hurts your chances, right?

 **REMINDERS:** Plan ahead and have plenty of matches, kindling, and firewood, and don't forget to bring camping chairs, blankets (just in case!), and eating utensils.

# 15.

## Iron Chef: Home Kitchen Edition
### $10–$25

**THE WHAT:** If you haven't ever seen an episode of *Iron Chef* or *Chopped*, look up clips on YouTube to get a sense of how they work. You have two options: (1) Before your date, pick three random ingredients from the grocery store, and buy two of each. Try to be creative and use at least one out-of-the-norm item. Set a time limit and compete against your date to make the best meal out of the three ingredients and anything else you find in the kitchen. (2) Buy six servings of one very unusual food. This has to be the main ingredient in an appetizer, main course, and dessert, and you'll be competing against your partner to win each round. Once you're done, test out the dishes. If they're delicious, nice work! If they're awful, end the night by ordering a pizza.

**THE WHY:** A little friendly competition will get your companion actively involved, and the close quarters of the kitchen will give you ample opportunity to sabotage each other's cooking experiments and engage in a bit of harmless trash talk. In other words, this date is just plain fun.

 **FILM FANATICS:** After you've tried it yourself, watch a couple episodes of *Iron Chef* with your date and ogle over how simple the pros make it look.

 **GET YOUR GROUP ON:** Make this a double date by inviting another couple to join in! In this version, you and your partner would compete against the other couple to see who could make the best dish.

# 16. Sugar Pie Honey Bunch
## $5–$15

**THE WHAT:** When they're in season, pick berries or apples at a local farm or orchard. Get enough for a couple of pies or enough to freeze and last you the rest of the summer—it's up to you! Once home, make a pie or cobbler together. Top it with vanilla ice cream and enjoy, or make multiple to deliver to neighbors or loved ones.

**THE WHY:** There's something so organic and natural about picking your own produce and turning it into something that spreads joy. For many people, baking is inseparable from the love of a mother, grandmother, or other caretaker, and this date may be a good opportunity to get to know about your partner's relationship with his or her immediate family.

 **THE FILM FANATIC:** Pies play minor roles in a number of movies, but they rose to comedic stardom in *The Help,* a fantastic movie about race relations in 1960s Mississippi.

# 17. Let's Do Brunch

$10–$25

**THE WHAT:** After sleeping in on a Saturday or Sunday, invite your date over to make a gourmet brunch. Together, prepare crepes, waffles, French toast, eggs benedict, bacon, sausage, fresh fruit, juice, or anything your hearts desire (just make sure to have the grocery shopping done ahead of time!). Eat until you're stuffed and then take an afternoon stroll, go window shopping, or just stay in and find something to pop in the DVD player. See how much of the movie you can make it through before you both fall into a food-induced coma.

**THE WHY:** We are constantly scheduling our days to the max, rushing from one place to next, leaving no time to just *relaaax*. You can plan this brunch as a miniature stay-cation after your partner has had a particularly stressful week, or just as a much-needed rest and recuperation time.

 **REMINDERS:** If this is one of your first dates with this person, check to find out about his or her food preferences or allergies before planning the menu. Better safe than sorry, and he or she will appreciate the gesture!

 **FILM FANATICS:** Rent *Breakfast at Tiffany's* and watch it together after you've eaten and feel too full to go out.

# 18. Restaurant Roulette

$15–$100

**THE WHAT:** Have a three-course dinner . . . at three different restaurants! Start with an appetizer at a café or sports grill, then move to a cozy restaurant for the entrée, and find the best pastry or cheesecake in town for the dessert. You can plan the restaurants by proximity, so that you can walk from one to the next, or pick your favorites regardless of location and enjoy the drives. The best part is that this date can be adjusted to fit your budget, high or low—you could dine at three different fast food restaurants or spring for a five-course culinary experience.

**THE WHY:** Everyone loves food, so dinner dates seem like a natural choice. But they can also get boring or awkward, fast. By switching between restaurants for each course, you'll get a change of scenery and, with it, a fresh start to your conversation three times throughout the night.

 **KEEP IT CHEAP:** You don't have to spend a lot of money to have a good time. If you're short on cash, grab french fries as your appetizer, a slice of pizza as your entrée, and an ice cream cone for dessert. You want to date someone who appreciates *you*, so any partner that seems put off by your spending situation probably isn't right for you anyway.

# 19.

## Do You Fondue?

$10–$30

**THE WHAT:** A sudden fad in the 1970s, fondue is the Swiss practice of melting cheese or chocolate and using skewers to dip various small foods like pieces of bread or bits of fruits and vegetables into the mixture. While it's used mainly for appetizers and desserts, you can also use a hot broth fondue to cook vegetables and meats as a main course. If you don't already own a fondue pot, you can often pick them up for cheap at a secondhand store or simply use any stove-safe ceramic bowl and a candle or other heat source.

**THE WHY:** Fondue is a great excuse to turn the lights down low, break out the candles and the mood music, and just enjoy a quiet night together. It's low-key while still being something fun and new. Plus, it's delicious, and you can't argue with that.

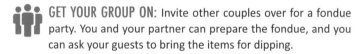 **GET YOUR GROUP ON:** Invite other couples over for a fondue party. You and your partner can prepare the fondue, and you can ask your guests to bring the items for dipping.

# 20. Pizza with Personality
## $8–$25

**THE WHAT:** Bust out the pizza stone and get to work creating masterpieces! Buy premade pizza dough or make your own the night before. With your partner, decorate full or individual-sized pizzas. Use toppings like pepperoni, bell peppers, onions, pineapple, and tomato chunks to make a picture or pattern or spell out words. Cook according to the directions on the premade dough or dough recipe, and enjoy! Or make several small pizzas to deliver to friends, complete with personalized pictures or messages.

**THE WHY:** Dinner dates can be a great way to work your social life into your schedule—you both need to make and eat dinner, so you might as well do it together and make a night out of it.

 **REMINDERS:** If this is one of your first dates with this person, check to find out about her food preferences or allergies before planning the menu. Better safe than sorry, and your date will appreciate the gesture!

# 21. Courageous Cuisine
## $5–$10

**THE WHAT:** Go to a grocery store, outdoor market, or Asian market, and pick out some fruits or vegetables that you've never seen, heard of, or tried before (like dragonfruit, lychee, or starfruit, for example). Buy them and bring them back to your house for a taste test. Experiment with cooking or preparing them in different ways, or look up recipes online that include them as an ingredient.

**THE WHY:** We spend a huge portion of our lives eating, and often eating the same few things that we've become accustomed to. This date is a chance for you and your partner to step outside that culinary comfort zone and get a "taste" for a few new things. Who knows, maybe you'll even like them!

**TALKING TIPS:** What's the strangest thing your date has ever eaten? If he had to eat only one food for the rest of his life, what would it be? What's the best meal he's ever had? The worst?

# 22. Taste Test

$5–$20

**THE WHAT:** Pick one food or drink item (root beer, apples, raspberry yogurt, whatever) and buy one of every type or brand of it. Go back to your house and do a blind taste test where you blindfold your date and feed her each brand one at a time. She'll rate each variety, and then you'll switch and you'll be the one doing the tasting. When you're finished, compare your ratings and determine your favorites—did you agree on the best brand?

**THE WHY:** If you've ever wondered what the difference was between the six brands of French vanilla ice cream at the grocery store, now's your chance to find out! It's a silly thing to do on a Saturday night, but it's also practical—now you'll be able to say with certainty that Gala is your favorite type of apple!

 **REMINDER:** This activity won't take very long, so it's a great date if you have a busy schedule or are just starting to get to know someone. If you want to make a longer evening out of it, do the taste test for multiple types of food or make it into a dinner event where you try different salad dressings, cuts of pork, and cupcake flavors.

# 23. Krispy Creations
## $5

**THE WHAT:** This date starts with a fresh batch of rice krispy treats. If you make them before your date comes over, make sure to time it so that the treats are nearly cooled but still malleable when she arrives. Otherwise, make them together and play a board or card game while you wait for them to sufficiently cool. When they're ready, lay a disposable table cloth or some newspaper down on the table and pull the batch out of the pan. Using toothpicks and the marshmallows' natural adhesion, create rice krispy treats sculptures! After the sculpture has hardened a bit, you can use a knife to carve smaller details. Have fun and get creative—your only limit is your imagination!

**THE WHY:** Most of us go weeks or even months without really kicking our creativity into high gear—we let it lie dormant while we focus on more practical matters. By forcing you and your date to more hands-on, this date gets your artistic juices flowing and creates a perfect right-brained bonding experience.

**BONUS:** Check out art books from the library or surf the web for inspiration for your own sculptures. Browse sites while you wait for the treats to cool.

# 24. Incredible Edible Cars
## $5–$20

**THE WHAT:** A favorite project among high school physics teachers, building an edible car also makes a unique date! The concept is simple: using only food items (and a little hot glue), create a functioning model car that only needs a push to get moving. Be observant at the grocery store and buy a variety of items that might work as car parts, getting several options in case one doesn't pan out. For example, you may want to buy Pixi Stix, spaghetti noodles, and pirouette cookies to try as axles. Make sure you have items to use to build the frame, wheel casings, axles, and wheels. Once you've found a design that works, celebrate your triumph by snacking on any leftover car parts.

**THE WHY:** As you and your partner put your heads together to find the best design for your car, you'll get a sense of how well you communicate and listen to each other's ideas and how differently or similarly you think.

 **GET YOUR GROUP ON:** Invite another couple or two over and make it a race to see who can get their car up and running first.

 **FILM FANATICS:** What better way to end your car date than by watching a movie about them? Pixar's *Cars* is an obvious choice, but *Speed Racer, Gone in 60 Seconds,* or *The Italian Job* are also great options.

# 25. Creative Cooking

$0–$15

**THE WHAT:** For this date, you and your partner are going to make dinner. What's the catch, you ask? No planning and no recipes allowed! Using only what you already have in your pantry and fridge, concoct a meal. If one course doesn't go as planned, start from scratch until you've made a decent dinner. If everything is truly awful, laugh about it and order takeout.

**THE WHY:** We've all been there—too lazy, tired, or busy to go to the grocery store and left with a few odds and ends to make dinner. This date is like training for those days, and a great way to practice getting creative in the kitchen.

 **TALKING TIPS:** You'll have plenty to talk about as you try to work together to transform a few basic ingredients into something scrumptious—just let the conversation flow naturally!

 **FILM FANATICS:** Once you've finished eating (whether it's the meal of your own creation or the daily special from Domino's), watch *Julie & Julia,* which is the story of a blogger's attempt to follow in Julia Child's famous culinary footsteps.

# 26. Sample Saturday

$0

**THE WHAT:** Go to Costco or Whole Foods on a Saturday and walk around the store trying the free vendor samples. See how many you can get from each cart before they recognize you and get suspicious. Go on a day that you really need to restock on some essentials, and invite your date to get her grocery shopping done too.

**THE WHY:** Dating is about getting to know someone, and that includes getting to know his or her everyday routine and habits. Not every date has to be a big, lavish affair—as long as you're spending time together and having fun, a little practicality is okay!

 **REMINDERS:** This date is not recommended as a first through fifth date—those earliest dates are the time to do the most planning and make the best impression. You don't want your date to think that you took her grocery shopping because you couldn't think of anything better to do.

# THE ARTS

# 27. Museum Magic
$0–$40

**THE WHAT:** Go to a museum. Any type of museum (science, art, history, cultural) will do—the point is to get out of the house and get cultured. Explore the exhibits together, talk about which ones you like and don't like and why, and get to know your partner's tastes and smarts. If it's an art museum, bring two sketchpads and pencils and spend some time trying to copy your favorite pieces on paper. Alternately, bring a camera and try to re-create portraits or sculptures by mimicking the facial expressions and poses of the subjects.

**THE WHY:** The exhibits in museums are symbols of our collective experiences. Works of art are depictions of the artist's understanding of life and what it means to be human. Science and history exhibits show us the world around us, condensed into digestible bits. With so much to see and analyze, it's almost impossible for conversation to run dry at a museum. You'll both leave feeling satisfied at having connected over something meaningful.

 **REMINDERS:** It's important that your date feels comfortable expressing his or her own opinion about the exhibits and the ideas presented—this is not the time to get into an argument or debate.

 **KEEP IT CHEAP:** Many museums offer free or "pay-what-you-can" Sundays, or other special deals. Look up these policies ahead of time and save some money by planning your date for one of these days.

# 28. Beatnik Buddies

$0–$15

**THE WHAT:** Attend a poetry reading or open-mic night at a local bookstore or coffee house. If you're feeling extra brave, dress up like beatniks in all black with berets and try your hand on the open mic. If your poetry is terrible, at least you'll have a great story to tell!

**THE WHY:** We all dream of being with someone who accepts us for who we are, but we have to take the first step by *showing* that person who we are. This activity is a great way to step out of your shell and let your guard down a little bit by being silly and okay with it.

 **REMINDERS:** There's an unwritten rule that if you attend an event at a restaurant, you should always order something. Coffeehouses and other establishments often offer to host these events in the hope that it will drive business, so please pay for the privilege by ordering off the menu and tipping your waitstaff well.

**GET YOUR GROUP ON:** Host your own poetry night at your house and invite a few other couples to attend! Ask everyone to dress up beatnik style, have paper and pens for people to write their own poetry, and keep a bongo drum handy to give the night more authenticity. The more outlandish and off-the-wall, the better!

# 29. Karaoke Cuties

$5–$20

**THE WHAT:** Find a local karaoke bar or restaurant that hosts karaoke and sing your hearts out! Sign up for as many rock ballad duets as you can before people start throwing things. Or, if your date isn't shy, each of you can sing solo.

**THE WHY:** This date is a great way to gauge how comfortable your date is in the limelight. Does she love having all eyes on her, or does she avoid it at all costs? If you're an outgoing person who likes to be the center of attention, this activity will help you get a better sense of whether your partner will keep up with you socially or shy away from similar events in the future.

 **REMINDERS:** Check to make sure your companion is up to the challenge of singing in front of people *before* the date. There's nothing more awkward than finding out when you get there that she would rather be anywhere else.

**GET YOUR GROUP ON:** The more friends who are in your corner for karaoke, the better. It's not about sounding good, it's about having fun, so showing up with your own personal cheering section will give you the confidence you need to belt it out in front of a room full of strangers, no matter what your voice sounds like.

# 30. CD Swap

$0

**THE WHAT:** Ask your date to create a mix CD (or tape, if you're old school) filled with his favorite songs, artists, or around a theme of his choice, and you'll do the same. For the date, get together and spend a couple of hours listening to each of your CDs. Pause before each song and explain why you chose to include it, and then listen to it, pausing wherever you feel to talk about the parts of the lyrics or music that especially impact you.

**THE WHY:** If you and your partner are music lovers, this date has the potential to be one of the best ever. The songs will bring out stories about when you first discovered the band, or the crazy concert you went to, or how one song got you through a bad breakup a few years ago. You'll find yourselves sharing silly, serious, and heartfelt memories and getting to know each other in a new way.

**REMINDERS:** There is such a thing as too much information in the early stages of dating. If this is one of your first dates with this partner, avoid including music that is tied to anything traumatic or personal that you're not yet ready to share.

# 31. The Drive-In Date

$10–$30

**THE WHAT:** They're becoming more scarce, but many towns still have an old drive-in movie theater, which makes a great alternative to a typical night at the movies or staying home with a rental. Tickets are usually comparable in price to the regular theater, but you don't have to pay exorbitant amounts for the theater's concessions because you can bring in your own! Have fun with it—bring a whole pizza or microwave your own popcorn ahead of time. Plus, it's easier to get cuddly in the privacy of your own car, and you can talk all you want without having to worry about disturbing your neighbors.

**THE WHY:** There is a certain charm to mom-and-pop grocery stores, 1950s-style ice cream parlors, and drive-in movie theaters that just makes you nostalgic for America's glory days. Experience a blast from the past and see what a date might have been like in your parents' or grandparents' day.

 **KEEP IT CHEAP:** Check for two-for-one deals or weeknight specials—drive-ins often offer off-peak prices for Monday–Thursday nights.

# 32. Drama Queen

## $10–$50

**THE WHAT:** Attend a play or musical at a small local theater, university, or high school. Several events are running at any given time, and you can check your local newspaper or online for reviews to decide which one best suits your and your date's interests.

**THE WHY:** Going to a play or musical is a totally different experience than watching a film, and it's a nice break from watching rentals on your couch or hitting up the local movie theater for the third weekend in a row. Plus, it feels good to give back to the community or support the ambitions of aspiring actors.

 **REMINDERS:** Make sure you've read a thorough synopsis of the play's content to ensure that it doesn't contain anything that will make you or your date uncomfortable.

 **KEEP IT CHEAP:** Theaters often offer discounts for students and have special pricing for matinee or weekday showings.

# 33. Find a Festival
## $50–$300

**THE WHAT:** Look up local film or music festivals and spend a day enjoying the arts and the atmosphere. These all-day affairs are like a modern version of Woodstock, with thousands of twenty-somethings congregating to bask in the "vibe." Often featuring both well-known and up-and-coming bands or directors, these festivals are an excellent chance to try something new without all the risk involved in attending indie events. If you're feeling really ambitious, make matching band T-shirts to wear to the show.

**THE WHY:** If you and your date are big music or movie buffs, there's no better way to bond than by getting out and enjoying what you love together. The day's ever-changing lineup creates a steady stream of things to talk about but also provides the chance to sit back and just enjoy the show should the conversation run dry.

 **REMINDERS:** You may find that you've bitten off more than you can chew if you try planning this as a first or second date. In the early stages of dating, while you and your partner are still unsure of your potential, avoid long activities, which may end up feeling forced.

 **GET YOUR GROUP ON:** To curtail the possible awkwardness of a lengthy date, invite other couples along to help the conversation flow more naturally. Bring camping chairs, blankets, and snacks, and take care to observe how your partner interacts in group situations.

# 34. Make Your Own Movie Theater
## $15–$80

**THE WHAT:** Using PVC pipe as a frame and a large white bedsheet as a screen, create your own backyard entertainment center. Borrow or rent a projector, set up outside, and have the popcorn, candy, and soda ready when your date arrives. Once it gets dark, settle in to camping chairs or the couch that you moved outside—you'll have the theater all to yourselves!

**THE WHY:** As a general rule, going out to the movies doesn't make a great date. But taking the initiative to build your own outdoor theater shows your date that you're interested in her in a way that dropping $10 for a ticket just doesn't.

**REMINDERS:** Check with your date before picking a movie to watch together. Don't assume that she likes chick flicks, or that he's into action movies.

**GET YOUR GROUP ON:** Make it a true theater experience by setting up a couple more rows of seats and inviting more couples along for the cinematic event of the year.

# 35. Make a Scene
## $0–$5

**THE WHAT:** Rent or stream an old, cheesy movie (*Godzilla vs. Mothra* or *Tremors,* for example) or one that you've seen a thousand times. Pop some popcorn, put the movie on mute, and make up an entirely new plot and dialogue as you go. If you've even seen *Mystery Science Theater* or *RiffTrax*, you know how this goes.

**THE WHY:** This is an interactive way to watch a movie that involves talking and laughing through the whole thing in an environment where you won't get shushed. If you fancy yourself the "funny guy" or the class clown, and you know your date enjoys being silly, this could be a great activity for the two of you to let loose and show off your stuff.

 **REMINDERS:** This date could get awkward really quickly if you or your date are the self-conscious type who don't like a lot of attention—this date is all about making a scene—literally!

# 36. Book Buddies

$0–$15

**THE WHAT:** If you're a self-proclaimed book nerd (as in you spend more time with fictional characters than with real people), attending a "reading" can be an excellent way to share your interest in literature with your date. Local authors or authors who are visiting on a book tour will often hold readings at bookstores or libraries—check who's coming to town soon and get to the venue early to get a good seat. There's usually no charge for these types of events, but buying the book is a sign of courtesy.

**THE WHY:** Gauge your date's interest in the activity while you're there—is she captivated or snoring by the second chapter? You don't have to call it quits if she doesn't share your passion for books, but it may be a sign that you'll need to try a little harder to find common interests.

**REMINDERS:** Make sure that you're familiar with the author you're going to see, or that you have at least researched the book's content. Nothing like showing up to a book reading to listen to an hour of a Victorian alien romance novel.

**FILM FANATICS:** Pick up a copy of *You've Got Mail* and watch it together once you get home. One of the classic Tom Hanks/Meg Ryan romantic comedies, this film takes place largely in a small corner bookstore.

# ARTS & CRAFTS

# 37. Blank Slate

$5–$30

**THE WHAT:** Buy a canvas in any size and bring out the paints, pencils, and glitter—it's craft time! Spend some time planning with your date how you want to use the blank space, and then get to work. Divide and conquer or work as a team until you're satisfied with the finished product.

**THE WHY:** This is your chance to see how artistic your date is, as well as how well you work as a team on creative projects. Are you on the same wavelength, or was it a struggle to agree on how to use your space? Does one of you take charge while the other sits back, or were you contributing equally?

 **KEEP IT CHEAP:** Instead of buying a canvas, use poster board. Or get a long piece of white butcher paper and create a wall-long mural!

# 38. Tee Time

## $10–$15

**THE WHAT:** Head to the craft store together and buy blank T-shirts and fabric craft supplies. Back at your house, decorate *each other's* T-shirts—use paint, Sharpies, glitter, puff paint, spray paint, iron-ons, and whatever else you can find, and have fun individualizing the shirt for your partner. They can be flirty like "I'm with the stud," have graffiti art, or incorporate inside jokes. Get creative with it and, most important, enjoy each other's company. Once you're finished, go out somewhere, anywhere, and show off your shirts!

**THE WHY:** The transition from being single to suddenly being part of a "couple" can be a very strange shift. This date helps ease some of that tension as it encourages you to get out and be seen together in a very public way.

 **KEEP IT CHEAP:** Use one of your old blank tees and ask your partner to bring one for himself that he wouldn't mind parting with. Most people have a couple in their closets that they'd be happy to put to better use.

# 39. Hands On

$10–$100

**THE WHAT:** Ask around at your community rec center or a local art studio about one-day pottery or sculpture workshops. Take your date and have a blast creating something new out of clay. The best part is that you'll have a new bowl or decoration to take home at the end of the day!

**THE WHY:** It's inevitable that when you try something new together, you'll have plenty to talk about as you navigate the experience. And while your pottery session probably won't end like the scene from *Ghost,* it could still be the beginning of something great.

**KEEP IT CHEAP:** Buy a hunk of clay from the craft supply store, put down newspaper on your kitchen table, and make your own sculpture studio at home! Check the label on the clay you buy—some of them can be baked in a home oven.

**FILM FANATICS:** As mentioned earlier, the Demi Moore/Patrick Swayze movie *Ghost* features a rather steamy pottery scene. If you're not in the mood for a post-mortal love story (though I can't imagine why that would be the case), you may be out of luck. Not a lot of movies about sculpture out there, it turns out.

# 40. Free Fair All

$0–$20

**THE WHAT:** Take your date to a local craft market or street fair and wander around the booths. If you're short on money, don't worry about buying anything—just enjoy checking out all the vendors. If you do have a little cash to spare, spring for tacos or an elephant ear, and come home with a keepsake. Getting your caricature drawn is fun and the picture makes a great souvenir from your date!

**THE WHY:** Carnivals, fairs, and markets are all about the *atmosphere.* Just take it in as you walk and talk, pointing out things that catch your eye. This activity can be especially enjoyable if you and your date are people-watchers.

 **KEEP IT CHEAP:** If you and your partner are past the early stages of dating and are a bit more comfortable together, create your own mini-fair at home. Cook up hot dogs and funnel cakes, watch YouTube videos that teach you how to juggle, and try your hand at drawing each other's caricatures (no hard feelings, right?).

# 41. Home Sweet Home

$0

**THE WHAT:** Volunteer with a local chapter of Habitat for Humanity or a similar organization that help build housing for the underprivileged. You and your date will have a great time getting to know each other while working with your hands for a good cause.

**THE WHY:** Almost everything we do every day centers around ourselves, so this date is an opportunity to step away from the "me" factor for a moment and concentrate on your community and those around you. You and your partner will connect on a deeper, more altruistic level as you come together to help others.

 **BONUS:** You get to see how good your companion looks in a hard hat.

# 42. Picture This

$0–$5

**THE WHAT:** Grab a DSLR camera (borrow one from a friend if you don't have a camera with manual settings), a tripod (or sturdy stool), and a couple of flashlights or glow sticks and create long-exposure light paintings. Make sure that it's very dark outside, set your exposure for a relatively long time, click the shutter release button, and use your light source to spell out your names or draw a simple image, or simply dance around and see how they turn out. Look at the recorded image afterward to make sure it worked—if not, the aperture or shutter speed may need additional adjustments.

**THE WHY:** There's always a thrill in having to wait for something—remember before digital cameras when you had to wait for your film to be developed and see how the pictures turned out? Taking long-exposure photos, especially on a non-digital camera, will bring back that excitement. And, assuming the date goes well (and how could it not?), you'll love looking back at the photos every now and again.

 **BONUS:** Once things start getting serious with this particular partner, you can start a photo album with all of your exploits in it.

# 43. Alternative Art
$0

**THE WHAT:** Using only things you already have in your house, plus a ton of hot glue, create custom sculptures or collages. Have paper and pencils available when your date arrives, and spend fifteen minutes or so planning and sketching out what you each want to make. Then scour the house for small disposable items that will work with the design. Think outside the box! Paperclips, toilet paper rolls, and plastic straws can make great building materials, and discarded magazines or fabric scraps will go a long way in decorating your creation.

**THE WHY:** This activity is pure creation—you get to make anything you want out of anything you want! It will facilitate talking as you and your partner discuss the finer points of egg cartons and bubble wrap and explain your finished products to each other. It's also completely free, unless you need to buy a glue gun.

**REMINDERS:** We were all blessed with different levels of artistic abilities and confidence in those abilities. If you're an artist by trade and your date is not artistically inclined, this may not make the best date, as she may feel upstaged by your creative prowess. But if she's got a good sense of humor about her own shortcomings, go for it!

# 44. Paper Play
$0

**THE WHAT:** Check out a book about paper airplanes from your local library. Gather a variety of papers (plain white, newspaper, magazine, wrapping, scrapbooking) and go to town building every one in the book—you can even try designing a few of your own. Decorate them using colored markers and pencils, and experiment with weighting the nose or wings using paperclips. Walk to a local park or an upper-story window and test each one out, noting which designs fly the longest and straightest.

**THE WHY:** You've both probably used the same standard paper airplane design your entire lives. This date combines teamwork and creativity as you design and decorate dozens of planes, and it will have you trying something totally new. And, who knows? Maybe you'll find a new go-to design to teach your kids someday.

 **FILM FANATICS:** *Top Gun, The Aviator,* or *Amelia* are all great choices for flying and plane-related flicks to watch once your paper-airplane-throwing arm gets tired.

# 45. Boxy Bonding

$0

**THE WHAT:** Build something awesome out of a big cardboard box. It could be functional, like your own giant Scrabble board or wall decorations, or something just for fun, like a spaceship, race car, robot, supercomputer, or the My Size Barbie you always wanted but never got for Christmas as a kid.

**THE WHY:** Similar to the "alternative art" date, this activity will really get your creative juices flowing as you start with a cardboard box as a blank canvas. You could build something together, promoting communication and teamwork, or separately, and enjoy peeking in on what the other person is working on.

 **TALKING TIPS:** What were some of your date's favorite make-believe stories as a child? Did he daydream about dinosaurs? Robots? Monster trucks? Have any of them carried over and become interests in his adult life as well?

# FUN & GAMES

# 46. Golf Galore

### $10–$20

**THE WHAT:** Head out to driving range, get a bucket of balls and some clubs, and go nuts. If you and your date have never golfed before, enlist the help of a staff member or the person on the neighboring platform and pick up a few techniques. Make the day more fun by wearing a visor, polo, and khaki shorts so you'll fit right in.

**THE WHY:** If it's the first time for both of you, you get to learn something new together without feeling out of place on the golf course. If you golf regularly, this would be a good low-stress way to introduce her to some of the basics without committing her to play a full eighteen holes. Plus, you can get up close and personal as you teach her how to swing.

 **FILM FANATICS:** *The Greatest Game Ever Played,* starring Shia LeBeouf, and *Happy Gilmore,* starring Adam Sandler, are two fun yet very different picks for finishing off your golf extravaganza.

# 47. Game Day
## $10–$100

**THE WHAT:** Attend a local sports game. High school football games are a great, cheap option and are excellent conversation starters as each of you talks about your high school days. College athletics, city or minor leagues, or professional sports are also good options. You can tailor this activity to your interests—soccer, hockey, football, or baseball games, tennis or racquetball matches, or track meets are all fun, budget-friendly events.

**THE WHY:** Sports games promote ever-changing and sustained conversation, since, when you run out of personal things to talk about, you can switch to talking about the game itself. There can also be thrilling moments when the team you're rooting for scores and the entire crowd erupts in celebration. Your partner may just get caught up in the commotion and oblige when the kiss-cam focuses in on the two of you.

 **REMINDERS:** Don't assume that your date has any interest or knowledge whatsoever of sports or of a specific sport—ask if he or she'd be interested in going to a game *before* you shell out for tickets.

 **FILM FANATICS:** Pick a movie that complements the game you just went to see. *Fever Pitch* or *Field of Dreams* are good baseball picks, whereas *Remember the Titans* or *The Blind Side* are great for football. Check out *Miracle* for hockey and *Hoosiers* for basketball.

# 48. Always Amusing

$20–$200

**THE WHAT:** Pick a small local amusement park or a larger one, if there's one in your area and within your budget. Ride the rides, scream and hold hands, buy an ice cream cone, win a stuffed animal—the whole shebang.

**THE WHY:** You never get too old for roller coasters and cotton candy! It's nearly impossible *not* to have a good time at an amusement park, so if you're looking for a no-fail first date, this is the one.

 **BONUS:** The top of a Ferris wheel or roller coaster makes for the perfect first kiss location and a great story.

 **KEEP IT CHEAP:** Check the park's website for promotions and discounts—you can often get half-day rates and discounts right as the seasons begin to change and the weather cools off.

 **REMINDERS:** Some people are more prone to motion sickness than others—check with your date to make sure he or she's okay with roller coasters and other thrill rides. Nothing kills the mood like throwing up.

# 49. Roll with It

$10–$30

**THE WHAT:** Roller-skating rinks are much fewer in number these days than in their 1970s heyday, but there a still a few around. Find one nearby and get your skate on! Most rinks give you the option of skates or blades—I recommend going retro and renting skates. If you're feeling daring, the two of you can dress up in disco gear. After you've had your fill, go out for ice cream or a quick burger and shake.

**THE WHY:** Unless you were a pro on the roller-skating circuit in the 1970s, you probably haven't spent any significant amount of time roller-skating. It's something new to do together and may be the perfect opportunity to grab your date's hand as you skate by.

 **KEEP IT CHEAP:** Check the rink's website or call in and ask about daily special deals. Many will have discounted rates on certain days or during certain hours.

# 50. Road Runners

$15–$40

**THE WHAT:** Find a local go-kart track and race, bump, turn, and speed your way to the finish line. Once probably won't be enough, so plan on buying enough tickets for two or more rides. Go-karts are often a part of larger parks that include miniature golf, bumper cars, batting cages, or small roller coaster rides, so bring a little extra money in case you and your partner feel like trying out anything else the venue has to offer. Afterward, spend some time chatting over a casual dinner or dessert.

**THE WHY:** It's just plain fun. That being said, sitting in separate go-karts isn't exactly conducive to conversation, so it's important to go out to eat or back to your place to hang out afterward so you can unwind and learn something about each other.

 **TALKING TIPS:** Has your partner ever been to Disneyland or a similar park? What memories does he have of family vacations, or what was his favorite one ever? Does he enjoy driving, or it more of a chore? What road trips has he been on?

# 51. Sweeping for Sport
## $10–$40

**THE WHAT:** Everybody knows about ice skating and hockey, but a glimpse at the Winter Olympics will tell you that a host of other winter sports rarely get any consideration. Curling is a sport that can be picked up fairly easily, and it's sometimes played at the same ice rinks where you would go skating. Kind of like shuffleboard on ice, the sport consists of one team member sliding a large stone down the ice toward a target while two others furiously "sweep" the ice in front of it to reduce friction and help it land on target. Read up on or look up YouTube videos about how the sport works, then research local rinks that run curling programs. Often you can join beginner classes that teach you the fundamentals and then let you play a few rounds at the end.

**THE WHY:** If you or your date enjoy ice skating or other cold-weather sports, you're bound to love curling. It's a slippery, slidey, and totally stellar way to spend a Friday or Saturday night.

 **TALKING TIPS:** Most of the time, you'll be focused on learning how to play the sport and won't have to worry about making chit-chat. Should you find yourselves standing around for a minute, ask your companion about her other sports experiences. Does she prefer winter or summer sports? What's her favorite Olympic sport or the sports moment from history that always gives her chills?

# 52. And BINGO Was the Game-O
## $10–$20

**THE WHAT:** Bingo may conjure images of old people and chain-smokers, and that's not entirely a misconception, but it can also make a great late-night date. Take your partner to a local bingo hall, grab some cards and markers, and cross your fingers for a big win. The markers are reusable, so hold on to them for the next time you visit.

**THE WHY:** You're bound to run into some interesting characters (some of these people have been coming to the same bingo hall for twenty years), and nothing compares to the thrill of winning, or even coming close to winning. You and your partner will find yourselves laughing, shouting, and nearly crying when you come *so* close but get beat to BINGO by the eighty-year-old grandma at the table in front of you.

 **REMINDERS:** Bingo is technically a form of gambling, so make sure before your date that your partner is comfortable with playing.

 **KEEP IT CHEAP:** Instead of stopping at a bingo hall, volunteer to play this or board games at a local senior care center. Many of them have recreation hours and welcome volunteers.

# 53. Horsing Around

## $15–$40

**THE WHAT:** Find a local race track and watch the horse races. Even if you don't bet on any of the horses, you'll get a kick out of picking a favorite and cheering to the end. And if you do put a couple of bucks on it, it makes it that much more exciting.

**THE WHY:** Horse racing is packed with thrills and tense moments, with jockeys falling or horses edging each other out for the front position. It's easy to talk throughout the race, in between jumping out of your seats to cheer.

 **REMINDERS:** Your date may be opposed to the idea of horse races due to concerns about gambling or animal treatment. Always check with your date before planning the activity.

 **FILM FANATICS:** *Seabiscuit* or *Hidalgo* are modern but classic movies about horse racing.

# 54. Billiard Buddies

$0–$5

**THE WHAT:** Find a pool table (often there are free ones at rec centers, bars, or universities) and play a bit of pool. If you're feeling fancy, look up the rules to snooker and try something other than standard pool.

**THE WHY:** A bit of friendly competition will kick up your date's intensity level a notch, which can expedite the "getting to know you" process.

**GET YOUR GROUP ON:** Pool makes a great double date because you and your partner can make a team and challenge the other couple to a few games. Alternately, the four (or six, or however many of you) can play CUE, a game similar to basketball's HORSE. To play, you use only the black and white cue balls. One person starts with the white ball in hand and the black ball is placed at the center of the far end of the table. From the opposite side, Player 1 has three chances to hit the black ball. If he fails, he gets a "C." If he succeeds in hitting the black ball, Player 2 grabs the white ball (which will now be ricocheting around the table) and attempts to hit the black ball (which is now also in motion). Player 2 must be on the opposite side of the table (you can only throw from the short ends) from the black ball when he rolls the white ball toward it, and the black ball cannot cross the center line of the table before the white ball hits it. If he succeeds, play continues the same for Player 3 and so on, always in the same order. If the black ball stops moving before a player is able to hit it with the white ball, that player receives a letter. Once a player has spelled CUE, he is out of the game, and the order of players shifts to accommodate him being out of the lineup. A player may also get a letter if the player immediately before him hits the black ball into one of the table's pockets before he is able to hit it.

# 55. Nickel Night

## $5–$15

**THE WHAT:** Visit a nickel arcade with a budget of around $5 each. Reminisce about favorite childhood games, defeat zombies and aliens together, and use your winnings to buy cheap knickknacks and candy.

**THE WHY:** Arcades are entertainment in their purest, cheapest form. For $5 you can play a ton of mindless, silly games and escape the stress of jobs and real life while you steer spaceships around meteors or drive jeeps through swarms of dinosaurs. You'll get to just laugh and relax together on a low-key, low-pressure date.

 **FILM FANATICS:** Rent *Wreck-It Ralph* for a fun and surprisingly hilarious animated glimpse into the world of arcade game characters. You won't be disappointed.

# 56. Derby Darlings
$10–$30

**THE WHAT:** Watch videos on YouTube to learn the basics of how roller derby works and then attend a local Roller Derby bout (most major and many minor cities have their own team). You'll soon pick favorite players and find yourselves using derby lingo in no time. Come up with your own derby names or pick them out for each other. I guarantee you'll become an instant fan.

**THE WHY:** Roller Derby was a by-product of the 1970s roller-skating craze, but it's stuck around, and for good reason. The all-women leagues include fun traditions like one-of-a-kind, punny derby names (like Devil Mae Clare or Relent-Leslie) and a uniform that usually incorporates fish-nets and mini skirts. It's like nothing either of you have ever seen before, and it's sure to be a good time.

 **FILM FANATICS:** Watch Ellen Page shine as Bliss Cavendar in Drew Barry's directorial debut, *Whip It.* Bliss is a small-town Texas girl who falls in love with Roller Derby despite her mother's wish for her to be a beauty pageant debutante. It's fast, fun, witty, and all about Roller Derby.

# 57. Eve of Destruction

$10–$40

**THE WHAT:** Forget whatever you learned about derbies from the previous date—this is a whole different ball game. In a demolition derby, people in junker cars drive around a dirt track trying to run into each other. They must take their first hit within a couple of minutes or get disqualified and, anytime they get hit, must return the favor and hit someone else within a couple of minutes as well. Rounds keep going until there is a finalist (or up to three) to move onto the next round. You'll see wheels fall off, tail pipes drag, and cars get high centered, flipped, or catch on fire—what's not to love?

**THE WHY:** If there's anything we can learn from *America's Funniest Videos*, it's that people love watching other people fall, crash, and collide. So what better way to bond with your date than over rednecks in stripped cars crashing into each other? It's like watching all of your favorite car-chase action scenes in quick succession.

 **TALKING TIPS:** What was your date's first car? What's his dream car? Has he ever been in a car accident? Gotten speeding tickets?

# 58. Rodeo Round-Up

### $15–$40

**THE WHAT:** Yee-haw, cowboy! If your county or state puts on an annual rodeo, scrounge around for your plaid shirt and big belt buckle and bring your date along. Rodeos typically host many events and contests, like calf roping, bull riding, barrel racing, team roping, and bronc riding.

**THE WHY:** Walking into a rodeo is like stepping into an entirely new culture for a few hours—one where big hair, big hats, big belt buckles, and big bulls reign. The entertainment doesn't stop for a second as one rider after another attempts to stay on board, and you and your partner will enjoy experiencing something so out of your norm.

 **FILM FANATICS:** Any good Western movie will do—go for a classic like *The Good, the Bad, and the Ugly* or any John Wayne movie, or something more recent like *Cowboys & Aliens* or the Coen brothers' remake of *True Grit.*

# 59. Ready, Aim, Fire!

$20

**THE WHAT:** Using surgical tubing for the force and a fabric pocket as the sling, build a water balloon launcher! Take it to a park, tie it between two posts or trees (or bring another couple along to hold the ends), stretch the pocket back, and let 'er rip! You can also build a giant target out of butcher paper or aim for various landmarks around the park (ten points for hitting the jogger!).

**THE WHY:** You and your companion will get a certain satisfaction out of creating something together, and this little baby will come in handy time and again in the summer.

 **GET YOUR GROUP ON:** Make this a double date by inviting another couple to make another launcher. Stand across the field from them and make it a competition—the first team to hit the other directly with a water balloon buys the other one milkshakes—no scooting out of the way at the last second!

# 60. Pinewood Partners

## $5–$10

**THE WHAT:** Purchase a pinewood derby kit (or two, if you each want to make your own car) and spend a couple of hours sawing, sanding, painting, and weighting your car to perfection. Create a makeshift ramp or find a slide to race them down. The fun is in making them, but it never hurts to get the bragging rights of winning either.

**THE WHY:** This date combines hands-on, artistic, and competitive aspects to create an all-around good time for you and your partner. You'll be amazed at how into it the two of you will get as your carve, paint, and race your miniature automobiles.

 **GET YOUR GROUP ON:** Plan in advance and invite another couple to be your competition. Spend a few dates working with your partner to craft the perfect car while your friends do the same, and then find a ramp and race them for the big finale.

**FILM FANATICS:** Find a copy of the 1994 movie *Little Rascals*. The big final scene involves a tense stock car race and a dramatic character reveal. Kid stuff, maybe, but also quality cinema. For those with more grown-up (read: boring) tastes, there's always 1965's *The Great Race*.

# ESPECIALLY FOR GROUPS

# 61. Paint Pals

$15–$25

**THE WHAT:** Buy (don't borrow) the game of Twister and washable children's paint in red, blue, yellow, and green. Make sure everyone knows to wear old, grubby clothing. Set the mat up outdoors on a patio or field and pour a bit of paint in the corresponding color onto each circle. After that it's Twister as usual, except that you'll be slipping, sliding, and transforming the mat (and each other) into a work of art as you go!

**THE WHY:** The more people that play Twister, the crazier it becomes, so it makes an excellent group date. You could even combine multiple mats to make a giant game. Because *everyone* is crowded in, this activity is a great chance to get close and test your chemistry without having to be too forward.

**REMINDER:** This game gets messy, fast. Make sure you set up near an outdoor faucet or hose so that you can spray yourselves and the mat down. For double the fun, get some soap and turn the mats into a slip-n-slide for easy cleanup and a perfect end to the date.

# 62. Team Tubing

$10–$30

**THE WHAT:** Find a friend with a pool or pay for entrance into a community swimming pool. Try to go at an hour when few others will be there. Buy individual inner tubes and, with a group of at least four couples, stage an inner tube water polo match. Call ahead to see if the pool has nets you can use. If not, fashion some makeshift ones out of overturned recycling bins, or make goal posts out of any two items that will stand up on their own.

**THE WHY:** Swimming always sounds like fun, but after a few minutes of showing off your perfect dive (or belly flop), you realize there's really not much more to do. So if you're looking for exercise or a way to cool off on a hot day *and* an opportunity to make a splash with your sweetie, inner tube water polo is just the thing.

 **FILM FANATICS:** An oldie but goodie, 1968's *The Swimmer* with Burt Lancaster tells the story of a man's determination to swim in every pool in his suburb until he makes it back to his own home, much to the consternation of his neighbors.

# 63. Food Fight
$0–$30

**THE WHAT:** Ever watched a movie where a food fight breaks out in the school cafeteria and thought, "awesome"? If so, this date is for you. Find an open field or space in a park, invite a few other couples, have everyone bring whatever they've got in their fridges, and go at it. Get creative—sloppy leftovers or things in squirt bottles or pressurized cans, like whipped cream or ketchup, are totally fair game.

**THE WHY:** Why not? Don't tell me you haven't always kind of wanted get caught in the middle of a food fight. Now's your chance to run around like a kid and make a good old fashioned mess. I guarantee you and your date will be laughing the whole time, and a relationship founded on fun is bound to go far.

 **REMINDER:** Make sure to wear old clothing and avoid overly sticky or hard food items like honey or apples.

 **FILM FANATICS:** Nineties family movies *Heavyweights* and *Hook* feature over-the-top food fights that may induce PTSD from your own recent culinary battle.

# 64. Cowboy, Take Me Away

## $15–50

**THE WHAT:** Make a bonfire on a brisk evening and dust off that Stetson—it's cowboy poetry night. Invite other couples to wear their best plaid shirts and spurred boots and bring along their favorite Western poetry, short stories, or folk songs. With a dutch oven of stew or cobbler cooking or with hot dogs roasting, share the stories by the light of the campfire and take in the stars and smell of pine around you.

**THE WHY:** There's just something about cold nights by the campfire that brings out the warmth in all of us. People open up, share, and laugh more around fire, and the structure of sharing favorite poems and songs ensures that you'll never run out of conversation.

 **REMINDER:** Remember to plan carefully and make sure that there's enough wood to keep the fire going for as long as you want to stay, and enough food to keep everybody happy.

# 65. Lovely Lawn Games
$10–$50

**THE WHAT:** On a day when the weather's cooperating, pair up, grab some friends, and play croquet, bocce ball, badminton, horseshoes, or other lawn games, using your date as your teammate. Borrow the games if you can, or look for used sets on Craigslist or eBay. Celebrate the points you win with a victory dance, have prizes ready for the champions, and come ready with lemonade and finger foods to keep everybody happy.

**THE WHY:** Lawn games are a great alternative to playing the same five board games week after week, or participating in more strenuous sports and physical activities. They'll get you outside enjoying the weather without forcing you to break a sweat, and they're slow-paced and casual enough to allow for conversation throughout.

 **BONUS:** This date is extra entertaining if you style it like an old-fashioned garden party, complete with wicker furniture and tea sets, and ask people to dress in their finest garden dresses and bow ties.

# 66. Capture the Flag Fun

$2–$20

**THE WHAT:** Invite your date and at least five other couples for a game of capture the flag—with a warm weather twist! Spend the morning filling buckets with water balloons and placing them around a field. Split the teams equally to start a game of capture the flag, with the following changes: (1) Instead of tagging you when you cross onto their side of the field, your opponents must hit you with a water balloon in order to capture you and put you in jail. (2) The "flag" that each team is guarding is actually a loaded water gun and whoever captures it may use it in self-defense at they try to make it back to their own home base.

**THE WHY:** Water games are a great way to cool off while simultaneously heating things up with your sweetheart, and they're sure to work up both your appetites so that you can seamlessly transition from the group date to a special dinner for two.

 **REMINDER:** Make sure to tell your date and the other couples to wear clothes and footwear that they don't mind getting wet, muddy, or grass stained.

# 67. Paint Your Partner Red

$30–$80

**THE WHAT:** If you and your date aren't afraid of a few bruises, paintball is an adrenaline-fueled adventure that you'll both be talking about for weeks afterward. Look up local paintball courses in your area and invite several other couples to come along. It's best to get a group of friends together so you can begin your own game right away and avoid having to play with strangers, many of whom may be much more experienced and trigger-happy than you are. You usually have the option of bringing your own equipment and paying an entrance fee, or renting the course's equipment and buying paintballs from them on top of the entrance fee. Last man standing, capture the flag, and last team standing are all easy, fun games to help you get acquainted with aim, strategy, and your partner's problem-solving skills all at once.

**THE WHY:** Sometimes, to have an *extra*ordinary date, you have to push yourself to do something out of the ordinary. Dinner and a movie are nice, but you're going to learn a lot more about your partner when you're relying on them for cover as you make a run through enemy territory than you are when you ask them to pass you the popcorn.

 **REMINDER:** Wear old, dark clothing (paintballs may stain), long sleeves and pants, and pick a day that's moderate, temperature-wise.

 **FILM FANATICS:** After a long day on the paintball battlefield, it would be only fitting to watch one of the great war movies: *The Longest Day* or episodes of *Band of Brothers* are excellent choices.

# 68. All In
## $5–$10

**THE WHAT:** Invite two or three other couples over for a rousing round of candy poker. Determine a value system (Tootsie Rolls = 1, Starbursts = 2, and mini chocolate bars = 5, for example) and let everyone know to bring a variety to bet with. Pick a type of poker (Texas Hold 'Em, five-card stud, and so on) and go over the rules before you start. You and your date can play as a team or enjoy calling each other's bluffs. At the end of the night, you'll have (hopefully) earned a big pile of candy and learned a big secret: your date's "tell."

**THE WHY:** Games are great, but to make things a little more interesting, all you have to do is put some chocolate on the line. You'll soon get insight into the inner workings of your partner's mind, not to mention figure out her favorite candy.

 **FILM FANATIC:** For some very involved poker scenes, *Casino Royale,* the 2006 James Bond film, is a great choice. The 2001 version of *Ocean's Eleven* takes place in several casinos and is a fun portrayal of the Las Vegas gambling scene. For something a bit more classic, *The Sting* with Paul Newman and Robert Redford features one of the most intricate and entertaining con stories in film history, and it all starts with a poker game.

# 69. Potluck Party

$5–$20

**THE WHAT:** Dinner parties are fun, but cooking for a large group can be a daunting task. Instead of making every dish yourselves, invite a few other couples to share in the fun! You and your date can make the main course, and assign the other couples to prepare side dishes, salads, beverages, or desserts. The dinner could be themed, like a luau or Mexican fiesta, or more casual, and you could combine it with a movie or game night. Serve, enjoy, and spend some time in good company.

**THE WHY:** This date is a great opportunity to spend both one-on-one and no-pressure group time with your partner. Start the evening more intimately cooking together and end it with friends and flowing conversation. While individual dates are important to get to know each other, it's just as important to understand who your date is around her friends or in larger social situations.

 **REMINDER:** Be sure to ask all of your invitees about food allergies or special dietary considerations, and make sure that everyone who is preparing a dish is aware of any issues.

# 70. White Water Wooing
## $50–$100

**THE WHAT:** Grab your sunblock and your sense of adventure—you're going rafting! If you live within a couple hours of a river, no summer activity is more thrilling than white water rafting. Find a reputable company with experienced guides, and invite a few other couples to join you on the river for a day of riding the rapids—it's more fun if you can fill the whole raft with friends. Plan on your trip taking at least six hours, between driving to the site, rafting, stopping for lunch, more rafting, and driving back home. At the end of the day, you'll be exhausted, in a good way.

**THE WHY:** There's nothing quite like the rush you get plunging headfirst into a class IV rapid, or the bond you feel with someone after experiencing near death with them.

 **REMINDER:** Safety is the number-one concern while rafting. Make it your personal priority to see that everyone is wearing properly fitting life vests.

 **PUNNY PICKUP LINE:** Do you like water? Then you already love 75 percent of me!

# 71. An In-Tents Adventure
## $15–$50

**THE WHAT:** Pick a state or national park within a couple hours of where you live, invite another couple or two along, and spend the night in the great outdoors. Plan out hiking routes ahead of time and divide responsibility for planning and paying for the various meals between the couples. Bring enough firewood to last the night and to cook breakfast, if necessary, and don't forget the lighter!

**THE WHY:** Camping is so versatile—you can pick a park with beautiful waterfalls, dense forest, red rock canyons, or vast meadows and have a different experience every time you go. Plus, do s'mores ever get old?

**FILM FANATICS:** If you're missing civilization, bring along a portable DVD player or laptop and pop in either version of *The Parent Trap* (1961 with Hayley Mills or 1998 with Lindsay Lohan), which both take place at a summer camp.

# CULTURAL AFFAIRS

# 72. Investigating India
## $15–$40

**THE WHAT:** Celebrate the world's second-most populous country by going out for Indian food (or ordering in) and watching a Bollywood movie. If you're new to Indian cuisine, try a curry, masala, or saag, and you can't go wrong. And don't forget the naan! If you're worried about the spice, most restaurants will give you the option of ordering the dish mild, medium, or hot—just ask! For the film, consider *Lagaan* (Indian citizens rise up against British rule through a high stakes cricket game) or *Barfi!* (the story of a hearing impaired man's search for love in a society that does not accept him).

**THE WHY:** Dinner and a movie is a classic date, but it can get old fast when you're eating and watching a lot of the same things. This date dares you to try new dishes and experience something new cinematically. Bollywood may be a bit of an acquired taste, often with over-the-top plot lines and big dance and musical numbers, but, at the very least, it will get you out of your comfort zone and provide plenty of talking points as you and your date notice the differences between India and your own culture.

 **BONUS:** If you're not shy, spend some time after the movie ends looking up traditional Indian dance videos on YouTube and trying to imitate the sweet moves you saw in the movie.

# 73. Paris, je t'aime
$10–$30

**THE WHAT:** France is known first and foremost for its gourmet food scene, so what better way to celebrate its culture than by cooking a really great, traditional French meal? If your culinary skills are minimal, omelets are a cheap, easy option, and baguettes, cheese, and chocolate are classic. If you and your date are up to a challenge, beef bourguignon, quiche, French onion soup, or ratatouille are delicious regional favorites. Cultivate the mood further by playing traditional accordion music during dinner.

**THE WHY:** Delicious food—need I say more? Okay, then how about this: Mac and cheese or sandwiches are fine, but planning and preparing a difficult or new recipe always brings with it a sense of accomplishment that you just don't get from a quick-fix dinner.

 **FILM FANATICS:** It may be a kid flick, but Disney Pixar's *Ratatouille* is a timeless take on the Parisian preoccupation with cooking as an art, and is just plain fun.

# 74. Hawaii at Home
## $10–$40

**THE WHAT:** Create a luau for two in your own home or backyard. Together with your date, cook traditional or popular Hawaiian items like pulled pork, rice, sweet potatoes, or dishes that include Spam or coconut milk. Then, find a tutorial online and use either fresh flowers or paper to create leis. Try your hand at the ukulele or put on some Hawaiian meles and take a shot at the hula. Grass skirts are encouraged.

**THE WHY:** Because you've always secretly wished you had a little more luau in your life, and because this gives you an excuse to make that happen. Also, studies show that whether your significant other looks good in a hula skirt is a strong indicator of marital success.*

 **FILM FANATICS:** Check out Disney's *Lilo and Stitch* or *South Pacific,* both of which take place in Hawaii.

*Studies do not actually show this.*

# 75. It's Amore
## $10–$30

**THE WHAT:** Decorate your dining or living room like a classic Italian eatery, complete with red-checkered tablecloths and host a pasta-heavy dinner for your sweetheart. For extra effect, try making your own pasta together, then go on a starlit gondola (canoe) ride and pay a friend to steer and/or sing and play for you.

**THE WHY:** We see birds singing, lovey-dovey romance in Hallmark commercials and chick flicks, but how often do we really get to experience that in real life? You'll give your date the time of her life by treating her to a special night that's straight out of the movies.

**TALKING TIPS:** Which parts of the world is your date most interested in visiting? Does she like lazy beach vacations, sightseeing tours, or high adventure?

**FILM FANATICS:** The obvious choice here is Disney's *Lady and the Tramp,* where the spaghetti scene may inspire you to make your own romantic moves.

# 76. Japanorama
## $0–$60

**THE WHAT:** There are lots of possibilities for creating a stellar Japanese culture night for your partner. If it's a dinnertime date, consider creating your own sushi rolls with seaweed paper, cooked rice, and crab or other seafood. For a night at home, provide a fun mix of colorful and patterned papers, rent an instructional book from the library, and create origami. Follow that up with a Japanese film (see recommendations below). If you'd rather get out of the house, find a local martial arts studio and enroll you and your date in a beginner's karate class.

**THE WHY:** You won't know if you like something until you've tried it, and you'll learn a lot about yourself and your date as you each respond to new situations. And if you end up hating sushi, finding origami tedious, and making a fool of yourself in karate class, at least you can say that you've tried them . . . and then add them to your mental list of things never to attempt again.

 **FILM FANATICS:** Japan is known for its unique style of animation, and Hayao Miyazaki's movies are among the most famous. Check out *My Neighbor Totoro* for a feel-good family movie. Or if you prefer something with more of an action edge, *Seven Samurai* is a classic of Japanese cinema.

# 77. Mexican Mash-Up

## $10–$50

**THE WHAT:** Create an authentic Mexican meal by making your own flour tortillas and loading them up with rice, beans, tomatoes or salsa, cheese, and chorizo or a meat of your choice. Mix up some horchata, and, for dessert, find a recipe online or in a book and try your hand at cooking sweet empanadas or making flan. Alternatively, if you're not big into cooking, find a local authentic Mexican restaurant (Taco Bell does not count) and order something you've never tried before. Back at home, use cardboard, an X-Acto knife, tape, crepe paper, and glue to design and create your own piñatas. They can be any size or shape you like—just fill them with candy and then either destroy them on the spot and eat it all right away, or save them for an upcoming occasion. Add to the mood with mariachi music and sombreros, if you like.

**THE WHY:** It's only polite to get to know your neighbors! For a more authentic experience, you can also check to see if your community has a Mexican or Latin American cultural center, or visit a Mexican mercado and incorporate some new items into your weekly grocery rotation. A positive community begins with cultural acceptance and understanding, which begins with you!

 **BONUS:** End the night with Latin dancing at a local club or attend a folk dancing class that covers the basics of traditional Mexican dances.

# 78. Candidly Canada

$5–$60

**THE WHAT:** Show your Canadian pride by taking your date to a game of either of Canada's national sports, lacrosse or hockey. If you're okay with spending a little more money, take your honey to a professional match. Otherwise, find a local university team to cheer on! Afterward, head back to your place for some flapjacks with real maple syrup, and watch your favorite Canadian Mountie save the day in a couple episodes of *Dudley Do-Right.*

**THE WHY:** This date is so varied and versatile that it's impossible *not* to have fun. Between sports, food, and cartoons, you should have all of your bases covered. And if sports aren't your thing, don't sweat it—this date is easily customizable by swapping hockey for ice skating and picking a different Canadian-themed movie.

 **TALKING TIPS:** What's the furthest outside the country that your date has traveled? Would he ever consider being an expat or moving abroad permanently? What factors are important to him when considering a move or a vacation?

# 79.

## Hometown Hubris

$20–$100

**THE WHAT:** Not all cultural adventures have to revolve around exotic locations—you can explore the culture of your own city or state by taking a daylong road trip through it! Plan a rough route (a loop) that will take four to six hours of driving time total, and then stop at anything that looks interesting along the way. Who knows what you'll stumble upon in your very own state—the world's largest potato? A vintage penny arcade? A wig shop? Stop at a hole-in-the wall restaurant for lunch or dinner and order a menu item you've never tried before—all in the name of exploration!

**THE WHY:** Everybody knows the major tourist attractions where they live, but it takes a concentrated effort to seek out and find the smaller, quainter charms of the culture of your city or state. You'll come away from this date feeling more connected to each other and the area where you live, and you may even find a new favorite spot in your own city.

 **TALKING TIPS:** You may have lots of time to kill in the car—in addition to pointing out and talking about landmarks or areas of special significance to you, consider bringing along music, podcasts, or *The Book of Questions* (see page 164) to keep you occupied.

# SEASONAL & HOLIDAY

# 80. Hokey Holidays

$0–$?

**THE WHAT:** Life can get a little glum when entire months go by without any holidays or parties. Luckily every day is an obscure holiday just waiting to be celebrated! Using the calendar on daysoftheyear.com or an Internet search for "obscure holidays," find an upcoming holiday and build a date around it. October 8, for example, is "Face Your Fears Day," and you and your partner could each pick something you're afraid of to go out and conquer together. Or celebrate Dr. Seuss's birthday on March 2 by checking out every book by him at the local library and eating a lunch of green eggs and ham. The possibilities are only limited by the number of days in the year!

**THE WHY:** Because it doesn't need to be a special occasion for you to get out of the house and have a good time! Being alive is reason enough to celebrate, and these sometime silly, always exciting obscure holidays help you do just that.

 **FILM FANATICS:** A nationally recognized but still strange holiday, Groundhog Day on February 2 is the perfect excuse to do this date. Rent or borrow the Bill Murray film titled, you guessed it, *Groundhog Day,* and revel in the dark comedy as one man experiences the same day . . . day after day after day.

# 81. Baby, It's Cold Outside

$0–$5

**THE WHAT:** On a day with enough snow, bundle up and build a snowman together! You can go for the classic Frosty look, complete with coal eyes and top hat, or favor a more modern, abstract Calvin and Hobbes style. Share favorite "snow day" memories from your childhoods, if you lived in an area with snow, and just have fun with it! When you're finished or it gets too cold, whichever comes first, dash inside for some hot cocoa and cozy up under a flannel blanket to watch a movie or just enjoy each other's company.

**THE WHY:** The only thing more beautiful than a fresh snowfall is getting to enjoy it with someone you care about. Instead of trudging through the snow, stop everything and bask in it!

 **FILM FANATICS:** If you can find a copy of Nickelodeon's *Snow Day,* it's an adorable teenage tale about the magic of, well, snow days. Or if the holiday season is upon you, check out a Christmas classic like *A Christmas Story, It's A Wonderful Life,* or the more recent *Elf.*

# 82. Sugar Mama
## $5–$10

**THE WHAT:** Invite your sweetheart over to cook up a little something in the kitchen! Make and decorate sugar cookies or fudge to deliver to friends, family, neighbors, or strangers who look like they're having a hard day. Let loose and get messy in the kitchen, and enjoy stopping and chatting with the people you deliver the goodies to—you'll meet each other's loved ones along the way!

**THE WHY:** It feels good to give! As the television and magazines shout at you to consume more and hit every sale, you can counter all the materialism and get back to the true spirit of the holiday season with some good old-fashioned giving.

 **TALKING TIPS:** What treats and meals does your date's family always make during the holiday season? Does she have any secret family recipes she's taking to the grave? What's the nicest thing anybody ever did for her at this time of year?

# 83. Creepy Couple

$0–$10

**THE WHAT:** Around Halloween, find a spooky spot, like a cemetery or an abandoned house, to explore at night. Do grave rubbings, have a candlelight picnic, and tell ghost stories—see how long you can last without losing your cool and heading for the hills. Alternately, with a few fake cobwebs and some sound effects, you can turn your own home into a haunted house, and follow up the picnic with a horror movie.

**THE WHY:** Halloween can be a blast, but it can also be the same old party with the same people every year—why not mix it up a little bit by doing something new to kick it into Halloween high gear?

**REMINDER:** Always be respectful of private property and make sure that you have permission to use the location of your choice before staging this date.

**FILM FANATICS:** 1993's *Hocus Pocus* starring Bette Midler is still creepy two decades later, and 2007's *Stardust* features some pretty great witchcraft as well, but with the added bonus of a cute love story to keep your romantic atmosphere intact.

# 84. Mmm-Mmm Good
## $0

**THE WHAT:** You'll be warming things up a little, quite literally, with this date. Ask your date to accompany you to volunteer at a soup kitchen or homeless shelter during the holiday season to get into the true spirit of giving. Chat with each other, the patrons, and other volunteers and make an effort to brighten someone's day, and you won't even notice your knees complaining about the two hours on your feet. I guarantee you'll be so impressed with the experience that you'll want to incorporate it into your traditions every year.

**THE WHY:** Throughout your life, you've had people who nurtured you and raised you up when you needed a friend the most. In a small way, this date is an opportunity for you and your partner to be those people for others when *they* need it the most. It'll bring out the best in both of you, which is a great feeling when you're getting to know someone.

 **REMINDER:** Homeless shelters and other nonprofit organizations can always use extra hands at *any* time of year—you don't have to limit yourself to the holiday season.

# 85. A Very Merry Unbirthday
$10–$50

**THE WHAT:** If you've ever seen *Alice in Wonderland,* or read Lewis Carroll's *Through the Looking Glass,* you already know what I'm talking about. If not, here's the gist of it: an unbirthday is any day of the year other than your actual birthday, but it can be celebrated just the same! The best part is that an unbirthday can be anything you want it to be: throw a surprise unbirthday party for your partner by inviting all of his friends over ahead of time and preparing cake and presents as usual. He won't suspect a thing! Or put together a romantic night where you go out for gourmet dessert and exchange small gifts, or invite everyone whose birthday it's *not* over for cake and ice cream and games. Whatever you do, have fun with it! After all, not *every* day is an unbirthday!

**THE WHY:** Your *birthday* only comes once a year, and can often bring with it the sting of aging. An *unbirthday* has all the same elements but none of the pressure to throw a great party or get the perfect gift. It's the perfect excuse to kick back and eat cake without worrying about whether you're too old to rock those pink pants or how much longer you've got before the stores start giving you a senior discount.

 **TALKING TIPS:** What was your date's most memorable birthday? Why? What was the best birthday gift he ever received and who gave it to him?

# 86. O Tannenbaum

$5–$60

**THE WHAT:** Gather supplies and decorate a Christmas tree together! Whether you favor artificial or fresh-cut trees, after you and your date have gone to town with tinsel, string lights, and ornaments, you'll end with a masterpiece that will spread joy for weeks.

 **BONUS:** Create your own ornaments out of photos, figurines and string, popsicle sticks, or whatever you can find, and create truly personal decorations that you'll want hanging on your trees for years to come.

**THE WHY:** A large part of dating is gauging how well your partner fits into your life and your habits and traditions. When two people begin dating, they should never drop everything and make their lives about each other—rather, they should begin incorporating each other into their lives. This date, besides being pure holiday magic, is about introducing your date to some of your long-standing traditions and testing how well she fits into them.

 **KEEP IT CHEAP:** Can't afford to fork over the cash for a tree? No problem! Head down to a local park and decorate a tree there—it'll bring Christmas cheer to everyone who passes by and you can visit it as often as you like.

# 87. Slippery Slope

## $5–$20

**THE WHAT:** Pick up a couple of cheap sleds (or just one if you want an excuse to get cozy with your date) from Target or Walmart and head for the hills! On a snowy day, scout out the steepest spots in your neighborhood and hit them all. Try building simple ramps out of packed snow and see how much air you can get, or experiment with the type of sled you use—inner tubes and large cookie sheets can work just as well! Warm up afterward with some chicken noodle soup (bonus points if it's homemade) or hot apple cider.

**THE WHY:** There's a reason water parks and roller coaster rides are always packed in the summer—people can't get enough of that stomach-dropping, flying-faster-than-is-natural feeling. Sledding is a way to get that thrill for cheap in the off-season. Plus, there's nothing like hurtling down a steep hill together to make your honey want to hold on to you a little tighter.

 **KEEP IT CHEAP:** Lunch trays, trash can lids, and shovels can all work as sleds, and you can probably scrounge them up from around the house!

# 88. Recycle, Reduce, Reuse
## $1–$20

**THE WHAT:** Arbor Day often gets overlooked as a national holiday, but it's an occasion worth commemorating. On the final Friday in April (note that some states celebrate it at other times due to varying climate patterns), buy a seedling of a tree of your choice and, along with your partner, plant it in your yard or a publicly owned area. Planting won't take long, so follow it up with a hike in the great outdoors or an art project using only recyclable materials.

**THE WHY:** This is the date that keeps on giving. By planting a tree, you're contributing to a cleaner, greener environment for all of us. And, you can make this an annual date as you stop by your planting site each year on Arbor Day to check on your little tree.

 **THE PUNNY PICKUP LINE:** If you were a tree, I'd be a tree hugger.

# 89. An A-maize-ing Date
## $10–$30

**THE WHAT:** In the fall, corn mazes and pumpkin patches (which are often combined at one venue) make an awesome activity. Besides a chance to pick out a pumpkin, many local farms offer petting zoos, hay rides, corn mazes, and even mini train rides or bounce houses! Or, if you like to keep the creepy in Halloween, some offer haunted corn mazes after dark, where teenagers dressed as zombies and monsters chase you through a labyrinth as you run for your life. What could be better? Back home, bust out the carving tools and get to work making prizeworthy jack-o'-lanterns. If you're especially resourceful, you can save the guts and make pies or pumpkin bread.

**THE WHY:** Pumpkin patches may seem like kid stuff, but you'd be surprised once you get there how eager you are to find the perfect pumpkin, how much you adore baby goats, and how great it feels to sit next to your sweetie on the hay ride. Some things never get old.

 **FILM FANATICS:** It's hard to talk jack-o'-lanterns and Halloween without also mentioning Tim Burton's *The Nightmare Before Christmas,* which is a delightfully odd mix between the scare factor of Halloween and the gentle spirit of Christmas. It's the perfect transition into the holiday season.

# 90. Candy Castle
## $7–$20

**THE WHAT:** Another favorite childhood activity that never gets old, making gingerbread houses with your date is guaranteed to be messy, merry, and oh-so-sweet all at once. Using cardboard covered in aluminum foil or other paper for a base, graham crackers or homemade gingerbread for the walls, plenty of icing as glue, and various candies for the details, spend a night decorating gingerbread houses together. Sketch out a master blueprint ahead of time, if you like, or just start pasting and see what happens! Create a house together or work separately, and, at the end, stand back and admire your masterpiece. The candy will go stale fast, so I recommend taking a few pictures and then inviting your date over again a few nights later to devour your delicious handiwork. Or, if you'd rather, keep the houses on display all holiday season.

**THE WHY:** This date combines a few of everybody's favorite things—crafts, sweets, and time spent with someone you care about. You just can't go wrong.

 **REMINDERS:** Graham crackers are convenient but generally don't make the sturdiest foundation for your house. Try taping or hot gluing several cardboard milk or juice boxes to form the base of your house, and then pasting graham cracker around the perimeter. Also, some types of icing form better bonds than others—find a recipe for royal icing for something that hardens quickly and will act like a strong glue for your candy.

# 91. Santa Baby

$20–$40

**THE WHAT:** Get in the Christmas spirit by going to the mall and waiting in line with a crowd of mostly four-year-olds and their harried parents for an hour and get your picture taken with your date and Santa! It may not sound like all that much fun, and it's definitely not for the faint of heart, but getting to see the excitement of Christmas through the eyes of a child again is pure magic.

**THE WHY:** You'll come away from your date with a great photo keepsake—and get to impress every preschooler you meet by showing him proof that you know Santa Claus. After your photo op, you and your date can browse the mall and get some Christmas shopping done . . . see, this date isn't *totally* impractical!

 **TALKING TIPS:** When and how did your date find out that Santa Claus wasn't real? How did she react? How does she want to approach the Santa situation with her own kids?

 **REMINDER:** Be very careful about discussing this subject with children around!

 **FILM FANATICS:** There's a great scene in the 1990 blockbuster *Home Alone* where Kevin McAllister has a candid conversation with a knockoff Santa Claus—this movie is as heartwarming as it is hilarious, and it's worth watching every few years around the holiday season.

# 92. Foliage Fun

$0

**THE WHAT:** Find an elderly or disabled neighbor who could use some help raking leaves in the fall. Gather a couple of rakes (borrow them if you need to) and some large trash bags, and invite your date to help you do some good in the world. Raking is tedious, so you'll have time to talk, and I bet your neighbors won't mind at all if you take a few dives into the leaf pile before bagging it all up.

**THE WHY:** This simple act of service makes a great date for a number of reasons: (1) You'll be genuinely helping someone who needs it; (2) If you've got to do yard work, you might as well have some company; and (3) Your partner's willingness to help out and spend time doing some of the more mundane things is an excellent indicator of his or her character. A date who expects you to bend over backward entertaining and lavishing attention on him all of the time probably won't stick around when there's hard or just plain boring work to be done. You want to find someone who will be right by your side in everything, and this date is a great test of that commitment.

# 93. Rainbow Bright

$0–$20

**THE WHAT:** Sometime during December, take your date for a drive through your neighborhood or the fanciest part of town to look at all of the Christmas lights and displays. You can get out and walk around or just keep driving until you're all Christ-massed out. For extra fun, make a list of categories like "Most Over the Top," "Classiest," or "Most Original" ahead of time and try to spot the winners on your walk or drive. Some cities also set up elaborate light displays around a racetrack or in fun locations like zoos and you can pay an entrance fee to go check them out.

**THE WHY:** Most of us just hang a strand of lights from our roof, decorate our tree, and call it good, but it's always fun to witness when people go the extra mile to light up dark winter nights with Christmas cheer.

 **BONUS:** Get inspired by the amazing displays you've just witnessed, head to the store for some essentials, and put a little more oomph into your own Christmas lights this year. Your date can help you plan, hang, and troubleshoot, and together you can step back and be proud that you're now among the Christmas-decorating elite.

# BAD WEATHER
# & PLAN B

*For when something goes awry and you need a quick,
easy date to throw together last minute*

# 94. Animals Aplenty

$0

**THE WHAT:** Volunteer to help walk, play with, or care for pets at your local Humane Society or animal shelter. Most of the pets have been either lost or abandoned and could use some extra love, and most of their caretakers are inundated with new arrivals all the time and could use the extra help. And, when puppies are involved, how could you *not* have a good time?

**THE WHY:** Besides making a positive difference in the community, this date can help you gauge your date's interest in animals. If you're an animal lover and pets are important to you, you'll likely be most compatible with someone who shares that affinity.

 **REMINDER:** Before inviting your date out for this activity, make sure he or she isn't allergic to pet dander or fur.

 **FILM FANATICS:** *Homeward Bound, Babe, Lassie Come Home, Charlotte's Web,* or *101 Dalmatians* are all excellent choices for animal lovers.

# 95. Fab Fort

$0–$10

**THE WHAT:** Remember dragging out all of the chairs and sheets you could find and making pillow forts as a kid? This date is your chance to relive the glory days, only bigger and better: make the ceiling tall enough to stand comfortably, have cushions, blankets, and bean bags spread around, bring in all the junk food and board games you can handle, and even move lamps or the TV inside so you can stay up all night if you want to. It's all the fun of a fort without the worry of your parents telling you it's time to put the furniture back in place and get to bed.

**THE WHY:** Much like crafts or cooking, building a fort allows you and your partner to create something together, navigating ceiling cave-ins and blankets that don't *quite* stretch as far as you need them to, and then sit back and enjoy what you've made with a relaxed game of cards or a movie.

 **TALKING TIPS:** You'll spend most of your time talking about the best way to affix linens to dining room chairs, but in the rare moments of silence, you can ask your date about her favorite things to create as a kid. Did she make forts? Build with Legos? Or was she more of a Play-Doh gal?

# 96. Youthful You

$0

**THE WHAT:** Ask your date to bring his high school (or college) yearbook over and dust off yours. Spend some time looking through them together and pointing out the class clowns, homecoming queens, history teachers, and football coaches who made high school what it was. You'll be amazed at how many memories come spilling out as you talk, and how great it feels to get to know someone and let him know you.

**THE WHY:** Everyone is a collection of past, present, and future experiences—you can't know someone, truly, without knowing who he used to be, and this date begins to unearth a piece of that puzzle. That and looking through old photos is just plain fun.

 **FILM FANATIC:** Pick a movie that came out and was popular when you were in high school, whenever that was. For example, *Ferris Bueller's Day Off* is a classic from the 1980s, *Clueless* is a great choice from the 1990s, and *Mean Girls* is a top pick from the 2000s.

# 97. Teaching and Talking
$0–$?

**THE WHAT:** Pick a useful but unique skill that you have and teach it to your partner. It could be changing engine oil, crocheting, canning peaches, driving a stick shift, starting a fire without matches, or anything that you know how to do that your date doesn't. It's as simple as gathering the materials you'll need and getting started!

**THE WHY:** Everyone has special talents and skills, and part of dating is sharing them with each other. Your partner will love learning something new, conversation flows easily because it's centered around the tasks, and you'll feel satisfied knowing that the two of you had fun *and* learned something new on such a simple date. And next time, you can ask her to teach you one of her special skills!

**NOTE:** If people frequently use the word *impatient* to describe you, this may not be the best date to undertake. You want to make sure that your date feels comfortable going at her own pace as she's learning something totally new.

# 98. Thrifty Throwback

$0–$10

**THE WHAT:** Locate the closest Goodwill, DI, or Salvation Army and go clothes shopping—for each other! Pick a category like "1970s," "Preppy," or "Gothic" and get hunting for the perfect outfit for your date. Make them as horrendous or as glam as you want, and play as many rounds as you like—the only rule is that the other person *must* try on the outfit you've chosen for them, and photos *will* be taken. You can leave without buying any of it, or pick up something cheap to take with you as a souvenir.

**THE WHY:** This is a cheap, easy date to put together, and it's certain to have both of you laughing within minutes. Most people tend to stick to a few favorite wardrobe pieces and rarely venture into foreign territory when it comes to clothing, so this is a great way to loosen up and solve the mystery of what you would look like if you'd gotten really into the 1990s grunge scene.

 **TALKING TIPS:** Your date may stick to business casual or jeans and T-shirts these days, but what style was he into in middle school or high school? What was his worst fashion mishap?

# 99. Working at the Car Wash
## $0–$10

**THE WHAT:** Yes, it can be a tedious chore, but it can also be an excuse to spend some time outdoors and playfully splish and splash with your date. Ask your date to bring her car over on a warm (or at least not a cold) day, bust out the soap and buckets, and the two of you can wash your cars while spending quality time together.

**THE WHY:** Not everything can be big and exciting all the time—routine chores have to get done, so you might as well do them together and talk and laugh while you do.

 **BONUS:** To make this date especially memorable, take one of your cars off-roading in a muddy area for a couple of hours, and *then* bring it home to wash it. This date also works well for dogs who need a bath—let them romp in puddles to their heart's content and hose them off at home.

# 100. Love Letters
## $1–$5

THE WHAT: Spend a couple of hours writing letters to important people in your lives. Have some nice stationery, pens, envelopes, and stamps ready when your date comes over, and just start writing. Write your mom to say thanks for putting up with you as a teenager, your BFF to tell her about the hot date you're on at this very moment, or your old professor to let him know what you've done with your life. As you write, talk to your partner about who these people are and why they're important to you, and encourage him to do the same.

THE WHY: It can take weeks, months, and even years of dating someone before you really get to know his family, friends, and other loved ones. This date can be done in a couple of hours but will prove invaluable to your understanding of the people who have most shaped your partner into the person he is today.

REMINDER: Don't push your date too hard for information about his family or past, especially if it seems like there might be some emotional hang-ups there. Things will come out in time, as you become more comfortable and secure with each other.

# 101. Sparks Fly

$10–$30

**THE WHAT:** Buy a working used microwave from a thrift store or the classifieds, and put everything in it that your mother, and common sense, told you not to put into it. CDs, Christmas ornaments, bars of soap, marshmallows, grapes, and snack sized chip bags are all encouraged. You'll be disappointed you've been missing out on all the fun for all these years!

**THE WHY:** Once you're out of high school, zany science experiments are a thing of the past, so gone are the awesome days of baking soda and vinegar explosions or frog dissections. Admit it—you miss them. This date is a way to get safely experimental and ooh and ahh over the wonder of science again.

 **THE PUNNY PICKUP LINE:** Are you made of Copper and Tellurium? Because you are CuTe!

# 102. Fun Shui

$0–$?

**THE WHAT:** Check out books on interior design or feng shui from the library, and then spend a couple hours rearranging or redecorating a room or two in your house or your date's. You can use solely what you've already got to work with, or take a trip to IKEA or another home goods store to get some fresh materials.

**THE WHY:** When you're dating, you end up spending a lot of time in each other's houses and on each other's couches. This date helps you take the time to create a space that you'll both love to be in and can be proud of.

 **BONUS:** If you're both up to the challenge, you can undertake a longer home improvement project, like painting a room a new color, installing shelving, or updating the light fixtures to be more modern.

# 103. Shopping without Spending
## $0

**THE WHAT:** On a rainy or otherwise dreary day, liven things up by taking a trip to a local boutique, toy store, or curiosity shop. Big chains are great for low prices, but the antiquated charm of a family-owned, hole-in-the-wall boutique is something you don't get to experience often in our fast-paced world. Browse, wander, play with the toys, touch anything you want, and don't worry about the price tags—you're not there to buy, just to be together.

**THE WHY:** There are lots of beautiful things in this world. Sadly, it would take a fortune to buy all of them, but that doesn't mean you can't get out and enjoy them just the same. If you're feeling strapped for cash, window shopping can be a fun excuse to leave the house and find your motivation to start saving.

 **TALKING TIPS:** Did your date get an allowance as a kid? What did she spend the money on? What's something she's always dreamed of owning but is too practical to buy?

# 104. Creative Construction
## $0–$50

**THE WHAT:** If you've still got your old container of Legos stashed under your bed or in your parents' attic, now is the time to drag it out! Use your personal stash or look for a cheap set at a secondhand store or online and spend an hour or two just messing around with one of the most popular toys in history. Give each other building challenges, work together to make the coolest Lego castle in the history of Lego castles, or play a form of sculpture Pictionary where your partner has two minutes to build something of her choice while you try to guess what it is.

**THE WHY:** You'd be surprised how fun it can be to pull out these tiny building blocks, and how easy it is to be creative when you're using a new medium. If nothing else, this date is a fun way to spend a rainy hour while you wait for dinner or for the skies to clear so you can get outside.

 **TALKING TIPS:** Does you partner excel at one form of creativity over the others? What's the art or creative project that she's most proud of? Did she ever consider a career in an artistic field, and which one?

# 105. Coupon Calamity

$0–$?

**THE WHAT:** Gather weekly mailers, magazines, and newspapers, and have your computer handy. Invite your date over and spend some time scouring the ads and sites like Groupon for local coupons. Your date can include any activities you like, with the stipulation that you *must* use a coupon for all of them. So your evening may end up involving a drive across town to the Thai restaurant that's offering a two-for-one special, tickets to a half-price comedy show, and a movie rental that you got for $1 off—just sift through your coupons and go!

**THE WHY:** Dating can get expensive, especially if you're going out to eat and paying for an activity every week. There's no shame in making a point of saving money, and this date will convince you that you can have plenty of fun on a smaller budget.

 **GET YOUR GROUP ON:** Tell other couples to sort through their junk mail and clip the same coupons, and then go out all together for the best budget-friendly night ever.

# 106. The Letter Is the Law

$0–$?

**THE WHAT:** Using a die from the game Scattergories or a bag of Scrabble tiles (or even just running your finger along a keyboard), pick a letter of the alphabet at random. The activities for your date must begin with that letter. So if you picked *K*, you may fly kites, kiss, eat Kit Kats, and so on. It may require some thinking outside the box, especially if you pull a letter like *X*, but keep to the letter as much as possible. Alternately, you could choose three different letters and pick three activities, one for each of the letters.

**THE WHY:** Counterintuitive as it sounds, sometimes spontaneity needs to be thought out and worked into a schedule ahead of time. This date allows you to be a bit random without the problem of sitting around staring at each other saying, "What do you wanna do tonight?"

**BONUS:** Borrow of buy a copy of Scattergories or Scrabble (or use an online version) and play at the end of the night to continue your letter-themed date.

# 107. Bucket Buddy

$0

**THE WHAT:** Use a quiet afternoon or evening to sit down and write out your "bucket lists," or a list of the things you want to do or see before you die. No looking over each other's shoulders on this one—come up with a list entirely your own and then read them aloud to each other once you're finished, explaining each item and answering questions that your partner has.

**THE WHY:** How well can you know someone without knowing their hopes, dreams, and desires for his or her future? This date is an excellent way to experience at least a piece of who your partner wants to be and become.

 **BONUS:** Pick one item from each of your lists and start planning them in earnest, either as future date activities, or as something to slowly work toward.

 **FILM FANATICS:** Jack Nicholson and Morgan Freeman play two terminally ill men who are trying to cross as many things off of their to-do lists as possible before they die in 2007's *The Bucket List*.

# 108. Going for Gold
## $0–$10

**THE WHAT:** Spend an evening with a copy of the *Guinness Book of World Records* and pick a few to try to beat that can be undertaken in the comfort of your own home. How quickly can you eat a banana, how many clothespins can you fit on your face (a real record . . . ), or how long can you go without blinking? Or, if you're feeling romantic, try to beat the time for the longest recorded kiss.

**THE WHY:** You probably won't beat any records in a single night, but you can sure have a blast trying, and looking through the book together will spur all kinds of crazy conversation topics.

 **BONUS:** Look up YouTube clips of other people's attempts to beat world records.

# WALKING & TALKING

# 109. Memory Lane

$0–$20

**THE WHAT:** Ask your date to pick a place where she has history (a campus, old neighborhood, etc.) and explore it together by foot. As you walk, she'll be able to point out places where major (or minor) life events happened, and you'll get to know more about her life. If you pass her favorite eatery from way back when, offer to stop in and treat her, or if she points out a former favorite concert venue, pop in and see what's playing. Don't worry about keeping any sort of itinerary—just go with the flow, and I promise you'll be glad you did.

**THE WHY:** Most of the time dates are a cooperative effort, and you hope that you and your partner contribute equally to the conversation and ambiance, but every once in a while it's a good idea to just *listen*. When you do, your date will feel cared for and connected to you, and is more likely to open up to you in the future.

 **TALKING TIPS:** Even though this date is all about listening, you may have to prime the well with some well thought out questions. What is your date's favorite memory from this place? Did she meet anyone here who really changed her life? If she could change something about her time here, what would it be?

# 110. The Duck Dialogue

$1–$5

**THE WHAT:** Visit a local duck pond with your partner and take a pleasant walk around the perimeter while you feed the birds. Even though you've probably always done it, try to avoid feeding the ducks bread products, as bread has almost no nutritional value for them. Instead, bring spinach, broccoli, grapes, or other fresh produce.

**THE WHY:** The real point of the date is the talking, but feeding the ducks is an added bonus, and it's delightful to watch them swim and dive and come close for a taste. Many people have fond memories of visiting duck ponds as a child, and the setting can trigger great conversation about those experiences.

 **FILM FANATICS:** Alfred Hitchcock's *The Birds* is the obvious choice, but if you *don't* feel like having nightmares later, check out *Chicken Run* by the same creators who brought you the Wallace & Gromit series.

## 111. Take a Tour
### $0–$40

**THE WHAT:** Someone else will be doing most of the talking in this instance, but it's still a great excuse to go for a walk, and you and your partner can come home saying that you without a doubt learned something new that day. Find a local historic monument, battle site, interesting company, or other point of interest and arrange to take a walking tour of the premises. Many monuments are free to enter, but most require a small fee for a guided tour.

**THE WHY:** Education and learning should be lifelong pursuits, but it's easy to fall out of the habit once you're out of school. This date is one that will help you better yourselves while at the same time enhancing your relationship.

 **KEEP IT CHEAP:** Many museums and historical sites offer student or senior discounts, or sponsor free admissions once a month. By doing a little research before you go, you could save some money on your tour and spend it where it really counts instead . . . on a sweet treat to end the night!

# 112. Heads or Tails

$5–$30

**THE WHAT:** Start in front of your house, and flip two coins. Two heads, you take a right; two tails, you take a left; one of each, you stay straight (if you only have two options for which direction to go, only flip one coin). Continue with every new intersection you come to. With literal twists and turns along the way, this date will feel like half stroll in the park, half board game. You may end up in some shady places, right by your best friend's house, or just walking in circles—go with it! Choose an end time and, once you've hit it, eat at the next restaurant you see.

**THE WHY:** Walking and talking has never been so exciting! You'll be amazed at all of the places in your neighborhood you never knew existed, and the anticipation of each coin flip makes for an added level of stimulation every few minutes, which in turn keeps the conversation flowing.

**BONUS:** This date works well if you're driving too—same rules apply, and you'll be able to cover a lot more ground in the same time frame.

# 113. Wild Life

$10–$35

**THE WHAT:** Visit your local zoo and stroll around the grounds together, making sure to hit all of your favorite exhibits and animals. As you walk and explore, talk about childhood memories at the zoo, funny experiences you've had with animals, books you've read about our similarities to apes—whatever comes to mind. Bring a camera to document your trip and snacks to munch on while you enjoy the views.

**THE WHY:** You may be surrounded by preschoolers and their harried parents, but the zoo holds charm even for adults. It's a chance to go on a safari without leaving your home state, and is a comfortable, easy place to walk, talk, and get to know each other.

 **FILM FANATICS:** *Life of Pi,* which won four Oscars in 2013, chronicles the story of an Indian family and their traveling zoo, and one boy's strained but special relationship with a tiger, and 2011's *We Bought a Zoo* is about a young family in California who, you guessed it, buy and repair a zoo. Either would be an excellent choice after this date.

# 114. Training Wheels

## $0–$40

**THE WHAT:** Sign up for a 5k or 10k walk/run with your partner and then prepare for race day by training together. Schedule a weekly jogging date and explore new paths, trails, or city blocks each time. Map routes that slowly work up to the full distance of the race, and time yourselves to check your progress. Wear matching shirts on the day of the race (you can even make them yourselves for a different date night), come prepared with plenty of water, and try to beat your personal record, together.

**THE WHY:** Your training time will become a cherished time of the week, and, even if you both turn out to prefer running in silence, it will bring you closer together through a mutual sense of accomplishment.

 **REMINDER:** If you and your date are at different levels of physical fitness, be considerate while running. He or she probably won't want to be left in the dust as you speed toward the finish line, and hopefully would give you the same consideration if the situation is reversed. Running, just like life, is more fun together!

 **TALKING TIPS:** If you are able to and enjoy talking while you jog, ask your date what her greatest physical accomplishment has been. What does she enjoy most about exercise? What forms of exercise could you not *pay* her to participate in?

129

# 115. Map Mayhem
$0–$40

**THE WHAT:** Find or purchase a map of your city and a couple of darts. Pin the map to a bulletin board, and take aim! You and your date will each throw a dart (or two, if you're really adventurous) at the map and then either drive, walk, or bike to those areas of the city and start exploring. Plan to grab a bite to eat wherever the first dart lands, and then hopping over to the second spot and going to a bowling alley, poetry reading, fabric store, or whatever looks most interesting to you. At the end of the night, you'll have found a couple new spots either to revisit or avoid like the plague.

**THE WHY:** We get stuck in our routines—we eat at the same places, stick around the same neighborhoods, and rarely venture into new areas, even ones that are nearby. This date will get you and your partner out of your rut and out and about experiencing new places.

 **TALKING TIPS:** What's the funniest or most bizarre situation your partner ever ended up in on accident? Is he the kind of person that seems to attract the crazy in life, or do most of his days stay pretty mellow? How is he with directions? What's the most lost he's ever been?

# 116. Playground Pals
### $0–$15

**THE WHAT:** Take your date to a local park or playground (bonus if it's one that either of you spent a lot of time at as kids) and swing, jump rope, play HORSE, draw with chalk, climb trees, and just generally get out and have some juvenile fun. If you feel like you're too old for those activities, go to a local park or playground that has particular significance to you, prepare a picnic, and sit back and enjoy watching the kids play.

**THE WHY:** It's important, while you're dating, to talk about each stage of your life with your partner. He may know you very well now, but to truly know someone takes time and a little bit more probing into the past that shaped them.

 **TALKING TIPS:** As you play or walk around the playground, memories of grade school friends and teachers, the science fair, or the time you broke your arm on the monkey bars will come flooding back. Let them come, and ask your date questions about her grade school experiences as well.

 **FILM FANATICS:** For a perfectly charming and silly look into the lives of the elementary school aged, look up old episodes of the cartoon show *Recess* on YouTube, or rent or stream the feature-length movie, *Recess: School's Out,* about a group of six fourth-graders who have to save their summer vacation from a rogue scientist and his ninjas.

# 117. Walking in a Winter Wonderland

## $0–$60

**THE WHAT:** Borrow or rent snowshoes, find a snow-covered slope, and get trekking! Many ski resorts rent snowshoes and offer Nordic areas that are prime for canvassing on foot, but any area with deep snow works. Dress in layers and bring a GPS device or compass if you plan to stray from main trails, as well as plenty of water and snacks. Your date can last for as little as an hour or could be an all-day adventure—the point is just to try something new and get moving! Afterward, put on a teakettle or make a stop at Starbucks for a warm beverage that'll put feeling back into your toes.

**THE WHY:** Snowshoeing makes a great winter date because it's a way to enjoy the great outdoors even in cold weather, and, unlike skiing, can be done at a nice, moderate pace that allows for ample breaks and conversation. If you and your date like hiking, you'll love snowshoeing!

 **FILM FANATICS:** *The Wildest Dream* is a visually stunning documentary that details the lives and exploits of two men who climbed Mount Everest. It'll make snowshoeing look like a walk in the park . . . which it kind of is.

# ROMANTIC

*__Warning:__ Many of these work best for married or established couples only, and should not be planned in the early stages of dating, lest you creep out the person you're trying so hard to impress.*

# 118. Surprise, Surprise
$0–$?

**THE WHAT:** Ask leading questions on an earlier date until your partner divulges a guilty pleasure (think 1990s pop music, *Star Trek*, crosswords, whatever), then plan a surprise date around that thing. Take him to see the Backstreet Boys reunion tour, go to a Trekkie convention, or track down every *New York Times* crossword from the year he was born and see how many you can get through together. This date is all about letting your romantic side out of the closet, so don't be afraid to go all out.

**THE WHY:** Relationships may be about partnership, but sometimes you just need to spoil each other. Your date will love that you're trying to share in his hobbies, and be flattered and touched that you took the initiative to plan something just for him.

 **KEEP IT CHEAP:** If you're strapped for cash and your partner's guilty pleasure is something expensive, like fine dining or front-row seats to pro ball games, don't be discouraged—be creative! Create a restaurant atmosphere at home and pick up the best cuts of steak at your local supermarket, or put together a montage of your partner's favorite team's best moments in sports history, pop some popcorn, and enjoy!

# 119. Falling in Love All Over Again
$0–$?

**THE WHAT:** Re-create your first date, revisit the location where you first met, first kissed, first said "I love you," or where you got engaged. If you know the date that it happened, surprise your partner and do it then. For a big milestone or wedding anniversary, do all of the above in one romantic, memory-filled date, if you can.

**THE WHY:** It's a common belief that the "infatuation" phase in relationships lasts only a couple of years, at which point partners settle into routines and no longer experience that heart-thumping, birds-singing, poetry-writing feeling that they did when they were first in love. We may settle into relationships as they progress, but that doesn't mean we have to lose that old feeling entirely. This date is the perfect excuse to act like a kid in love again, and, remembering those early experiences, you'll feel like one too.

 **TALKING TIPS:** What was running through your date's head the first time that you went out? That you kissed? When did she know that the two of you had something special? What has been her absolute favorite moment together?

# 120. Two to Tango

### $0–$15

**THE WHAT:** Even if you have two left feet, dancing is the language of love, and holding your date tight and whispering sweet nothings into her ear as you move to the music will bring the two of you closer together—in both senses. Many ballrooms or dance clubs have hour-long beginner's lessons before they open up the floor to the public, or you could clear a spot in the living room and practice along with instructional YouTube videos to get some steps down before you go. In most cities, you'll be able to find Latin (which is probably the easiest for beginners), ballroom, swing, and country-western venues—take your pick and kick up your heels!

**THE WHY:** Dancing is a great way to break the touch barrier, if you're still trying to figure out a way to hold your date's hand or get a bit closer. And if you're past that stage, it's a nice excuse to get a little dressed up and stay out late just loving on each other.

**FILM FANATICS:** Australian director Baz Luhrmann's *Strictly Ballroom,* about an unlikely ballroom dance pair, is laugh-out-loud funny, and the perfect way to end your night of dancing. *Mad Hot Ballroom,* a documentary about a dance competition featuring New York elementary school students, is another excellent choice.

# 121. Half and Half
$0–$?

**THE WHAT:** In this modern take on "going Dutch," you and your date will each plan half of the night, and keep your halves a complete secret from each other. Decide how to break the night into two segments ("you plan dinner, and I plan an activity," or "you take the first two hours and I take the second two"), and get plotting! You may end up both choosing mini golf, or going to a rodeo followed by a quiet night at an art museum—the combinations and possibilities are limitless, and you'll love not knowing what's happening next.

**THE WHY:** As a general rule of thumb, you shouldn't keep secrets from your significant other, but this rule is an awesome exception. Surprises add excitement to what might otherwise be a routine dinner and activity, and you'll each be on the edge of your seats waiting to see what the other has up his or her sleeve.

 **KEEP IT CHEAP:** To save a few bucks, stipulate that whatever each of you plans has to cost under $5, and let the creativity start flowing.

# 122. A Day at the Spa
## $0–$100

**THE WHAT:** This date is delightfully customizable! If you're married, go all out with an at-home spa day, complete with fuzzy robes, massages, and long showers. If you're not at that stage, consider manicures and pedicures; hand, foot, and head and neck massages; and facials. The point is to just *relax* and spend a day pampering yourselves.

**THE WHY:** Between work, school, getting dinner on the table, running errands, exercising, and who knows what else, it's easy to forget to make time for yourself and your partner. This date is about shutting off phones and the television, forgetting about the unfinished dishes, and completely enjoying the night.

 **REMINDER:** This date is for established or married couples only—do not attempt to plan this until you and your partner are completely comfortable with each other.

# 123. Rooftop Restaurant
### $10–$25

**THE WHAT:** It's dinner, elevated. Take your meal to an entirely new level, literally, by hosting dinner on a rooftop balcony or flat roof. Cook dinner beforehand and have it set up, complete with a little table, linens, and flatware when your date arrives. It's your chance to woo her under the stars and up and away from the world below.

**THE WHY:** Rooftops and balconies have an aura of romance about them that, while not entirely logical, has persisted since Romeo first caught sight of a pining Juliet through her second-story window.

 **FILM FANATICS:** Watch any film version of William Shakespeare's *Romeo and Juliet* after dinner for a romantic, if tragic, way to end the evening. My personal favorite is Baz Luhrman's 1996 adaptation.

# 124. Lyrical Love
## $10–$40

**THE WHAT:** Visit a dueling piano bar or other restaurant with a live musician. Tell your date you're going for appetizers or dinner and front the money to have the band or artist play "your song," as a surprise for your sweetie. If she's not easily embarrassed, pull her up front for a slow dance, to the applause of the crowd.

**THE WHY:** Music often has special meaning to relationships. The song you sang together on your first date to a karaoke bar, or the song that you danced to at your wedding can bring back a flood of wonderful memories of your earlier days together. The thoughtful surprise will make your partner feel loved and appreciated.

 **KEEP IT CHEAP:** Instead of shelling out for a professional to sing for your special someone, dust off the old guitar in the corner and start warming up the old vocal chords and serenade her yourself. Try standing at her window (bonus if she's got a balcony and you can sing up to her), or even using computer software to record your cover of the song. The time and energy you invest in practicing and performing will mean even more to her than hearing it from a professional.

# 125. Love Letters
$1–$3

**THE WHAT:** Break out the pretty stationery and pens and write love letters to each other. Remember your favorite moments together, write what you love about each other, and what you hope to do and be in the future. Seal the letters with a kiss or a spray of perfume or cologne, then mail them to each other and read them, together or separately, in a few days when they arrive. You'll fall in love all over again.

**THE WHY:** Couples get so in the habit of saying "I love you" that they may forget why they're really saying it. This date lets you focus on all of each other's excellent qualities and reminisce about the most special moments of your relationship. You'll come away from the activity with a renewed enthusiasm for the love you share.

 **BONUS:** Write multiple letters, and mail one every week or month until you run out (and then you could always write more!). Because who wouldn't enjoy opening the mailbox to find proof that they're loved?

# 126. Star Light Star Bright
## $0–$3

**THE WHAT:** Pick a clear night, find an open area, bring sleeping bags or blankets, hold hands, and look up at the stars as you talk about your hopes and dreams for the future. Bring constellations maps and locate as many as you can, or play connect-the-dots and find your own figures in the sky. Munch on Milky Ways or Little Debbie Star Crunch cakes for a sweet themed treat.

**THE WHY:** There's nothing like the vastness of the night sky to put your own life in perspective and talk about what you really want out of it. Something about lying out in the open will make you both want to *be* open, and you'll find yourselves sharing your innermost selves beneath the stars.

 **FILM FANATICS:** There are so many fantastic space-themed movies that you've probably already got a favorite, but if not, *Star Wars, Star Trek, Galaxy Quest, 2001: A Space Odyssey, Apollo 13,* and *Gravity* are all great places to start.

# 127. Love Languages

$0

**THE WHAT:** Borrow or check out a copy (or two) of *The 5 Love Languages: The Secret to Love That Lasts* by Gary D. Chapman. It's such a quick read that you and your partner could cozy up on the couch and get through it in an hour or two. Take the tests at the end of the book (there's one for men and one for women) and determine what your primary love languages are. Make guesses about your own and your partner's beforehand so you can have bragging rights if you guess correctly.

**THE WHY:** Relationships take work, but you might as well have fun while you work! The concepts in the book are easy to understand and implement, and will foster a greater awareness of each other's needs, so reading *The 5 Love Languages* is a win-win *and* a killer date night.

 **TALKING TIPS:** My guess is that you'll have plenty to talk about as you're reading the book and taking the tests, but once you've discovered your love languages, there may be kind of a "now what?" moment. Ask your partner for three ways that you could express love in his language that he would particularly value. Have you been oblivious to any of his most important needs? What activities does he think make for the best date night?

# 128. Water Water Everywhere

$0

**THE WHAT:** Go for a night swim together in a secluded pool, lake, or the ocean. Normally swimming spots are overcrowded with children, their anxious mothers, and foam noodles. Sneaking out to spend some one-on-one time in the relaxing still of the water is exactly the kind of spontaneous, youthful thing that chick flicks make us believe love is made of, and your date will fall head over heels for your devil-may-care charm.

**THE WHY:** To have great memories, you first have to *create* them. People don't often tell stories about the dates where they watched a movie and got ice cream because they probably weren't worth remembering. This activity is about making a date that is.

 **TALKING TIPS:** What's the most spontaneous thing your date has ever done? Was she nervous or exhilarated? Does she come from a family of impulsive or level-headed people?

# 129. Magically Delicious
$5–$20

**THE WHAT:** Make breakfast in bed for your darling, especially if he is feeling under the weather or could use a pick-me-up. Figure out his favorite foods to eat in the morning and set to work cooking up a crepe masterpiece or hearty helping of eggs and bacon. Bonus points if you squeeze your own orange juice. Serve on a tray (a cookie sheet will work in a pinch) complete with a vase and wildflower for the finishing touch. And, unless you enjoy watching other people eat, consider cooking up a little something for yourself too, so you can spend a lazy morning cuddling and stuffing yourselves silly.

**THE WHY:** You've heard that "the way to a man's heart is through his stomach," but the phrase is true for women too. People are less likely to be irritable and more likely to be warm and open once they've been fed. Plus, your partner will appreciate getting to take the morning off from cooking and doing dishes.

**GET YOUR GROUP ON:** For a special occasion or holiday, get a few couples involved in a breakfast bonanza! Encourage the women (or men) to spend the morning together while their better halves (that's you!) prepare breakfast or brunch and have it ready on their return. Then serve and enjoy, all together.

# LONG-DISTANCE LOVING

*Unfortunately, many couples find themselves having to date long distance at some point or another in their relationship. But the miles between you don't have to mean the end of quality time together.*

*Note: Wherever a film is recommended, it can be watched together long distance using the instructions in "(Don't) Silence Your Cell Phones" on page 153.*

# 130. Book Club
## $0–$15

**THE WHAT:** Pick a book that you've both been meaning to read, buy or check out a copy from the library, and create a reading schedule for yourselves. After each chapter or a certain number of pages, chat on the phone or over Skype about your favorite segments, characters, sentences, and other details.

**THE WHY:** When talking on the phone becomes your main method of communication, sometimes you need a little extra help finding topics to keep the conversation moving. Reading and analyzing the same book together will provoke deep, meaningful talks (and maybe even a few heated debates) that will help you get to know each other better on an intellectual plane.

 **FILM FANATICS:** If there's a movie adaptation of the book you're reading together, watch it after you've finished the last chapter. You can compare the book to the film and lament over how they totally cast the wrong actor for the lead. Or check out *The Diving Bell and the Butterfly* or *Stranger Than Fiction*, both of which are excellent and about authors struggling to write books.

# 131. Post Haste
$2–$8

**THE WHAT:** Spend an hour or two visiting gift shops in your town and finding the best, cutest, strangest, or prettiest postcards. Buy four and send one each week at a moment when you miss your sweetheart the most. Tell him what you're doing that day, which of his charms you find yourself pining for, or whatever else come to mind.

**THE WHY:** In this electronic age, it's so easy to send a text, email, or Facebook message letting someone know that you're thinking of him. But there's something reassuring and quaint about receiving a postcard that conveys that message a little better. And something as simple as your handwriting will be a welcome sight to your loved one after a long absence.

 **TALKING TIPS:** After he has received your postcards, talk to your partner on the phone about which was his favorite, and why. Has he ever gotten a life-changing letter in the mail (think college acceptance letter, pen pals, or correspondence from an aged relative).

# 132. We Be Jammin'

## $0–$2

**THE WHAT:** Ask your significant other to make a playlist of songs that remind her of you, and do the same but vice versa. Burn the songs onto a CD and send in the mail or send links to where you can listen to each other's lists. While on the phone, Skype, or a chatting system, listen to each song one by one and talk about why it holds particular value for you and your relationship. Was it the song you had stuck in your head the first time you met? Or do the lyrics remind you of her smile? If you haven't been together very long, it may be difficult to come up with a full playlist, so it's okay to each pick a "Top 5."

**THE WHY:** French and Spanish may be romance languages, but music is the language of romance. The way we relate to music and our favorite songs is something that's constantly running through our own heads and hearts, but that we rarely share with others. You'll let each other in a little bit more with this very personal date.

 **FILM FANATICS:** *Mr. Holland's Opus,* starring Richard Dreyfuss, is a heartbreaking but beautifully produced movie about a high school music teacher and his impact on his students.

# 133. Mad Gab about You

$0–$40

**THE WHAT:** You'll each need to borrow or buy a set of Mad Gab cards (check eBay for better deals). If you've never played before, here's the gist of it: Common phrases are separated phonetically and into other words, and it's your job to get your teammate to guess the real phrase. For example, "Lions and tigers and bears" might be written as "Lying sand tie girls ambers." You read it as written on the card, and your partner has to try to decipher it. Get on Skype or the phone and play—keep score or just go until your stomach hurts from laughing, and create fond memories even from afar.

**THE HOOK:** The stresses of long-distance relationships can begin to take their toll on a couple's collective mood, but you can combat the stress with the number one proven cure: the giggles.

**KEEP IT CHEAP:** Create your own phrases and try them out on each other—you'll get better as you go!

# 134. Christmas Come Early
## $5–$30

**THE WHAT:** Put together a care package for your partner and send it off as a sweet surprise. Include a picture of yourself (or a pillowcase printed with your picture for long-distance cuddles), comfort foods, love notes from you or friends, and other small trinkets or inside jokes that let him know you're thinking of him.

**THE WHY:** You've heard the phrase "talk is cheap." Unfortunately, when you're dating long distance, it can feel like talking is all you have to express your affection. Small gestures like this care package go a long way in showing, rather than telling, your love.

 **TALKING TIPS:** Once he's received your package and opened it up, your partner will probably call to say thanks and gush over how great you are. Revel in the gushing, and then ask what his favorite item was. If size and price weren't an issue, what would you include in an ultimate care package?

# 135. (Don't) Silence Your Cell Phones
## $0–$5

**THE WHAT:** Forget everything you've ever been told about talking or texting during movies—for this date, it's encouraged! Stream or rent a movie or TV series online, sit down to your computers, and watch something together. Use Skype (on mute), instant messaging, or texting to laugh, cry, or wonder about the same parts of the movie or show, so you'll really experience it together.

**THE WHY:** Long distance relationships will have lazy days where you just want to kick back, order pizza, and watch a movie like you would if you were together. And there's no reason you can't! Your favorite stay-at-home routines can and should be kept up even while you or your partner are far from home.

**GET YOUR GROUP ON:** Missing your friends or the other couples you used to hang out with together? Get them all involved in this stay-at-home date by inviting them to watch the same movie and join the same chat!

# 136. Giddy Gaming
## $0

**THE WHAT:** Similar to the last date, if you and your honey love staying in and playing Scrabble, cards, or video or other games, you still can! Most board and card games have online versions available for free, so you can continue taking out your competitive edges on each other, even from afar.

**THE WHY:** Long distance can really disrupt routines, and can be a big adjustment for couples who are used to spending a lot of quality time together. Make it as easy on yourselves as possible by incorporating as many of your "old standard" activities into your long-distance relationship as you can, and it'll be a smoother transition.

 **TALKING TIPS:** Whether you use Skype, instant messaging, or the phone, I recommend talking while you're playing games so that the activity better mimics normal (not long-distance) dating. Just talk about your day at work or school, how you regret wasting your blank tile on a fourteen-point word . . . whatever comes naturally!

# 137. Sing Your Heart Out
$0

**THE WHAT:** Using SingSnap.com or a similar online service, you can have a bona fide karaoke experience at home! The free website provides you with the music and the words—all you need is a warmed-up voice and a webcam, and you've got your very own karaoke music video that you can watch with your partner. Create and share with your date for a fun "night out" that you can do at home! Alternatively, you can find karaoke versions of most songs on YouTube. Turn your webcam on and perform them live for your sweetheart.

**THE WHY:** It can be rough—especially on a Friday night when all of your friends are out on dates—to be home wishing your partner lived closer and you could hit the town together. While the reality is that he or she doesn't and you can't, there's no harm in pretending that you're out on a date, singing your heart out for a room full of people.

 **BONUS:** Change out of your sweats, get dressed up, and throw on a little makeup or cologne for a more authentic date night experience.

# 138. Killer Personality

$0

**THE WHAT:** Find free online personality tests like the Myers-Briggs Type Indicator or the Color Code (Hartman) test and compare results. The Myers-Briggs examines four categories of personality traits, each with two variants, and assigns you a four-letter code that describes you in a nutshell. You can be introverted (I) or extroverted (E); sensing (S) or intuitive (N); thinking (T) or feeling (F); and judging (J) or perceiving (P). Color code tests ask you a series of questions or to agree with a series of statements that are supposed to discover your inner motivations. You can be red (a power wielder), blue (a do-gooder), white (a peacekeeper), or yellow (a fun lover). Once you each have your four-letter code or color, you can read the summaries of your personality types and laugh about how spot on the descriptions are, or look into what career options best suit your type. Google "personality test" for fun (albeit less professional) options like "What's my shoe personality?" or "Who's my inner celebrity?"

**THE WHY:** Yes, it probably sounds like a broken record by now, but *dating is about getting to know each other.* What better way to do that than by specifically analyzing your personalities?

# 139. Homemade with Love
## $5–$20

**THE WHAT:** Pick your date's favorite homemade snack and send it UPS or through a similar quick-shipping method. Make sure to choose something that will "keep" for at least a few days (cookies or dense breads like banana or zucchini are good options) and wrap it airtight in plastic wrap. Also make sure to use plenty of newspaper or packaging peanuts in the box, to avoid all of your hard work getting squished or crumbled on its journey.

**THE WHY:** When you live close to each other, it's easy to take the little things like holding hands or cooking together for granted. By picking a favorite homemade treat to send to your partner, you'll remind him of the little things that make life together so great.

 **TALKING TIPS:** What are the little things that each of you miss the most when you're far away from each other? What's the first thing that you want to do the next time you get to see each other?

# 140. Truth or Dare?

$0

**THE WHAT:** It may be the stereotypical "we're thirteen and at a sleepover" game, but Truth or Dare has its merits. If you somehow skipped over that awkward time of life, here are the rules: Flip a coin to see who gets to go first (no lying about the outcome just because your date can't see it!). The person who won the coin toss asks the other "Truth or Dare?" and he or she responds with their choice. For a "Truth," you get to ask your date *any* question, which must be answered honestly. For a "Dare," you get to challenge them to do any one thing. Be creative, but don't go overboard, and stay relatively within your date's comfort zone—remember, you're next!

**THE WHY:** Conversation can get stale when all you have to talk about is your boring day at school or the office. This date combats that problem by allowing you and your partner to ask personal questions that have absolutely nothing to do with sales reports or what you had for dinner.

 **REMINDER:** This date should only be undertaken once you and your partner are already quite comfortable with each other, and asking personal questions won't be *too* traumatizing . . .

# 141. Something New Every Day
$0

**THE WHAT:** Sign up for a free online course and listen to the lectures and study together. Many Ivy League schools offer video lecture series at no charge online. Topics range from Austrian economics to Hannibal to black holes and can be found simply by Googling "free online courses." I guarantee it'll be a refreshing experience, and that you'll both learn something new.

**THE WHY:** If you're still in school, this date may not seem like all that much fun. But if you're not, it's a great excuse to get those wheels turning again and connect with your partner on an intellectual level. And if the distance has dried up all of your best conversation topics, this activity will open up totally new avenues.

**THE PUNNY PICKUP LINE:** This textbook has got it all wrong—they forgot to include you in their list of the most important dates in history.

# 142. Final Countdown
## $0–$15

**THE WHAT:** Create a paper chain or wall calendar to mark off the days 'til you get the see each other again. Write things you love about your partner on each ring or each day, mark important anniversaries, and include favorite photos for each month. Send it to your honey as a sweet reminder that you can't wait to see them. Make a copy for yourself too!

**THE WHY:** Every day that passes is one that brings you closer to being together again—why not celebrate each little step?

 **KEEP IT CHEAP:** Instead of printing off and mailing a calendar, create one online using Google Calendar or a similar program.

# 143. "Long-Distance Life" for $600, Please, Alex

### $0–$10

**THE WHAT:** Take the questions from Trivial Pursuit, an old Jeopardy daily calendar, or any other trivia source (borrow or scour the Internet or eBay if you don't own these already), and take turns asking each other the questions over the phone or Skype. Don't go easy on each other and keep score—the loser has to air-mail a treat of the winner's choice, or has to plan your next date.

**THE WHY:** A little friendly competition will keep the two of you on your toes and out of the dull of the day-to-day, and you can't escape a trivia night without learning lots of new (if totally useless) facts. And who knows, maybe someone at the next party you're at will be impressed that you can name all of the presidential candidates from 1964.

 **TALKING TIPS:** Let the conversation align naturally with the trivia questions. If you think a new fact is interesting, stop the game to talk and wonder about it for a while—don't get so caught up in the points that you forget there's someone you care about on the other end of the line.

# 144. Silent Silliness

$0–$40

**THE WHAT:** If you haven't already invested in a webcam for your computer, get one now. You can pick a cheap one up for as little as $10, and getting to see your sweetheart's smiling face is well worth the investment. Using Skype or another video chatting service, play charades by taking turns acting out words or phrases silently and trying to get your partner to guess correctly. You can pick a category, like "movie titles" or "household objects," or jump around, and you should give yourself a time limit for each round. Keep score if you want to, or just play until you're laughing too hard to continue.

**THE WHY:** So much of someone's facial expressions, mannerisms, and other fun physical personality traits are lost during long distance when they become just a voice on the phone. This date, because you're not allowed to talk during much of it, combats that issue by letting you sit back and admire your partner as a whole, terrible Bugs Bunny impersonation and all.

 **TALKING TIPS:** The two of you probably do a lot of talking as is. Let this date be an occasion to just get to *see* and smile at each other (a lot), say good night, and feel good about where you are, without worrying about coming up with much to say.

# 145. A Pinteresting Date
$0

**THE WHAT:** Make sure that your date registers for a Pinterest account, and that you do the same (unless you want to share one), and then get pinning! Create boards that are solely focused on your relationship, like "Places we want to travel together," "Things to do when we see each other again," or "Recipes to try out together." You can also have a board where you just pin the best things you found on the Internet that day, whether it's a hilarious cat video on YouTube, a picture of that dress you want his opinion on, or a Shakespearean sonnet you thought was beautiful, and can comment on each other's pins.

**THE WHY:** Pinterest is a great way to keep up to date on the things that each of you is crushing on at the moment (besides each other, of course), and by having boards that are solely dedicated to the two of you, you'll feel like you're in an awesome secret club.

 **BONUS:** This date is ongoing, and can work around your individual schedules—just pin and comment when you can!

# 146. Q & A

$0–$15

**THE WHAT:** Borrow, check out from the library, or buy a copy of *The Book of Questions* by Gregory Stock and ask away! The more than 200 questions in the book include things like "Without your kidney as a transplant, someone close to you will die within one month. The odds that you will survive the operation are only 50 percent, but should you survive you would be certain of a normal life expectancy. Would you consent to the operation?" and "If you were guaranteed honest responses to any three questions, who would you question and what would you ask?"*

**THE WHY:** This date is a no-brainer in terms of great, stimulating conversation. You'll learn tons about your partner, her beliefs, and the inner workings of her mind as you pick questions at random and each answer honestly.

 **KEEP IT CHEAP:** If you've got the brain power for it, you can forgo getting the book and just take turns coming up with "would you rather" and other thought-provoking questions for each other.

*Gregory Stock, *The Book of Questions* (New York: Workman Publishing, 1987), 67, 179.

# 147. Podcast Puppy Love

$0

**THE WHAT:** While on instant messaging or Skype with the audio turned down, listen to a favorite podcast or watch a video in a series (think RadioLab or a TED Talk) at the same time, chatting about interesting segments as you go.

**THE WHY:** Like watching a movie or TV show long distance, this date lets you feel like you get to *do* and enjoy new things together again. And the best part is that it can turn into a beloved weekly ritual, if you find a podcast that you both love.

**GET YOUR GROUP ON:** There's no reason not to get your friends or other couples involved in this activity—pick a time that works for all of you, sign in to chat, press play, and let the conversation begin.

# 148. Can't Say No
## $5–$30

**THE WHAT:** Spend some time browsing at a local bookstore and pick up a copy of a book for your partner to read, and ask her to do the same for you. It could be an old favorite of yours that she's never read, or something that you've always meant to read one day but never gotten around to. Each of you will send each other your pick with a letter explaining why you chose it, and with the stipulation that you *have* to read whatever you receive within whatever time frame you set for yourselves. Once the deadline has passed, talk on the phone or over Skype about the book the other sent. Did you like it? What were your favorite or least favorite parts? Would you recommend it to a friend, and why or why not?

**THE WHY:** Every couple should have a system of checks and balances in place, where some nights it's time to suck it up and watch a chick flick with your partner, and others you have veto power. This date is a chance to bypass any vetoing rights you or your partner may have accrued, and share a book that's special or intriguing to each of you.

 **BONUS:** This date could also be done with movies, TV series, or music albums that you've always wished each other would at least *try* to appreciate.

# 149. Dream Lover
## $0–$25

**THE WHAT:** Borrow, check out from the library, or buy a dream dictionary and, over the phone or Skype, analyze your dreams. Dream dictionaries include an alphabetical list of objects and ideas and their symbolic meaning when found within the sleep state. So, for example, if your date has a recurring dream about turning into a white owl and flying over the forest at night, you could look up "white," "owl" or "bird," "forest," and "night" or "dark" and piece together an explanation of what his dream means on a real-life level. Do this for dreams you remember from your childhood, or ones you've had recently and see what your subconscious is trying to tell you.

**THE WHY:** While the accuracy and merit of dream interpretation is disputed, that doesn't stop the process from being fun! Maybe you'll be surprised at how relevant the symbolic meanings are in your life, or maybe you'll end up laughing over their absurdity. Either way, it's something new to try!

 **TALKING TIPS:** You'll find that this date is conducive to great conversation. As you rehash old dreams or nightmares, you'll end up telling each other stories about people and places from your pasts, and may find that you interpret certain items completely differently, and will get into a discussion about why you attach separate meanings to the same concepts.

# 150. The Language of Love
## $0

**THE WHAT:** Use duolingo.com or a similar free online language-learning program and get practicing! Pick a language that neither of you is familiar with, start with the beginner courses, and try to go at the same pace so you're learning together. Then, pick one day each week where you can only text or talk in that new language (or, when you're just starting out, where you incorporate new words and phrases into your regular conversations).

**THE WHY:** Learning new things, especially monumental ones like foreign languages, can be daunting. This date will keep both of you motivated, practiced, and excited about learning, and, if you keep at it long term, you'll come away with an awesome new skill to list on your résumé.

 **FILM FANATICS:** Find a movie that was filmed in the language you're trying to learn, and watch it together by keeping instant messaging open. Take a risk and watch it without subtitles to see how much you can understand, or turn them on and compare what you're hearing to the English on the screen.

**HALEY MILLER** has been going on a date a week for close to three years, which adds up to (you guessed it) right around 150 dates. Never one to give in to routine and mediocrity, Haley makes it a point to try something new every week, and this book is a record of her past adventures combined with her ever-growing bucket list. She holds a bachelor's degree in English with minors in editing and French, and currently works for a publishing house, which funds her dating life and fulfills her lifelong dream of reading for a living. Besides literature, Haley counts tennis, camping, TexMex, Paris, and her hometown of Portland, Oregon, among her most favorite things.